4-H GUIDE
TO TRAINING HORSES

Nathan Bowers and Katie Bowers Reiff

Voyageur Press

A portion of the sales of this product will be used to promote 4-H educational programs. No endorsement of this product by 4-H is implied or intended. Use of the 4-H Name & Emblem is authorized by USDA.

4-H is a community of six million young people across America learning leadership, citizenship, and life skills. National 4-H Council is the private sector, non-profit partner of National 4-H Headquarters (USDA). The 4-H programs are implemented by the 106 Land-Grant Universities and the Cooperative Extension System through their 3,100 local Extension offices across the country. Learn more about 4-H at www.4-H.org. 18 USC 707

WE DEDICATE THIS BOOK TO OUR DAD AND FRIEND, STEVE BOWERS.

First published in 2009 by Voyageur Press, an imprint of MBI Publishing Company, 400 First Avenue North, Suite 300, Minneapolis, MN 55401 USA

Voyageur Press titles are also available at discounts in bulk quantity for industrial or sales-promotional use. For details write to Special Sales Manager at MBI Publishing Company, 400 First Avenue North, Suite 300, Minneapolis, MN 55401 USA.

To find out more about our books, visit us online at www.voyageurpress.com.

Library of Congress Cataloging-in-Publication Data

Bowers, Nathan, 1988-
    4-H guide to training horses / Nathan Bowers and Katie Bowers Reiff. —
1st ed.
        p. cm.
    Includes index.
    ISBN 978-0-7603-3627-4 (flexibound)
    1. Horses—Training. I. Reiff, Katie Bowers, 1984- II. Title.
    SF287.B77 2010
    636.1'0835—dc22

                                                                    2009015299

Edited by Amy Glaser
Design Manager: Katie Sonmor
Series designed by Pauline Molinari
Layout by Danielle Carnito
Cover designed by the Book Designers
Front cover main photo: Mark J. Barrett, www.markjbarrett.com

Book reviewed by:
Bob Coleman, Ph.D. PAS

Printed in the United States of America

CONTENTS

DISCUSSION OF HORSES

This book is intended to be an overview and starting place for people who want to learn how to train horses. We hope you will learn a lot and that the information in this book will help you and your horse forge a stronger bond and a more meaningful relationship. We highly recommend that you continue your education beyond what you learn in this book. There are many great horsemen and -women in the world, and the best way to learn is to get opinions from these masters through additional books, DVDs, seminars, and lessons. The more effort you put into your horse training education, the faster and further you will be able to take the relationship with your horse.

For thousands of years, the horse has represented many things to humans. People first domesticated horses in Eurasia approximately six thousand years ago. Horses in the Americas experienced mass extinctions about 15,000 BC and were not reintroduced until Christopher Columbus brought them to the Americas on his second journey across the Atlantic in 1494. Modern-day wild horses in the Americas are actually descendants of domesticated horses that escaped or were turned loose by early settlers. In the initial years of domestication, the horse represented life and sustenance, as well as a weapon in warfare. Horses helped people increase the amount of goods they could make and the quantity of food they could raise and store. As time went on and people began to move about the land more, the horse became an important means of transportation. As people moved across the world, they set up boundaries and created estates and small countries. These small entities needed to protect themselves, and the horse proved to be a valuable weapon in warfare. It gave riders speed, agility, and an elevated view of the battlefield. Riders honed their riding skills and displayed them as local entertainment.

The more effort you put into your horse training education, the faster and further you will be able to take the relationship with your horse.

As you develop your relationship with your horse, you will start to notice that the horse responds to even the slightest pressure. This horse is responding to soft pressure across its nose by bending at the pole. This is a very nice response to pressure.

In the Old West, the horse was especially important in giving cowboys a way to watch over cattle. Horses helped open up the West and allowed the movement of people toward the Pacific. Along the way to the Pacific, early settlers also used the horse for cultivating the land, as well as mining. The movement of people increased the need for the movement of goods and food, so the horse was instrumental in the development of the United States. Everything that trucks, tractors, cars, trains, and airplanes do today, the horse did first. Since horses have played such a strategic role in history, it is no wonder

A true horseman or -woman will learn from as many wise people as possible. We are constantly learning and bettering ourselves, and we hope that you will do the same.

that they have turned into such a popular hobby, sport, and pastime for so many people. Now that the horse is no longer needed for mainstream transportation or farming, the horse and its trainer have become a romantic dream of the past. Those who currently

When we are training a horse, we don't want to shelter it. Notice that we are in an open area with all sorts of distractions, including a dog. Some people train their horses in a contained environment at all times and never allow the horse to be out in the open. By training your horse out in the open, your horse will be well seasoned and cultured by the time it is done with its basic training.

participate in this industry are becoming fewer and fewer, but hopefully, with the help of this book and similar materials, you will learn some of the ways of the past and present and will have success with your horse and horses in general.

The knowledge presented in this book has been gleaned by watching and learning from world-class horsemen such as Tom Dorrance, Bill Dorrance, Buck Brannaman, Curt Pate, Walter Zettl, Ray Hunt, Steve Bowers, and Pat Parelli. All these horsemen are legends in the horse industry, and we strongly encourage you to learn as much as you can from them so that you can become a better horse person. You will also find that the best teacher is the horse itself. There is no comparison to the knowledge you will gain from truly studying the horse. As you work with your horse, you may feel like you are training the horse, but remember that you are also learning. As you learn to relate to your horse, you will realize that the things you are learning about respect and relationships transfer directly over to your relationships with humans. A true horseman or -woman will learn from as many wise people as possible. We are constantly learning and bettering ourselves, and we hope that you will do the same.

We are asking this horse to respond to rein pressure by giving its nose. The horse is bracing against the rein pressure and not giving the response that was asked for. If this should happen with the horse you are working with, keep setting the horse up and asking it to respond to the rein pressure.

Giving a horse a job is an essential part of its education. It is extremely healthy to give the horse a sense of purpose so it doesn't feel as if it is something for you to simply play with. You will notice immediately that your horse's expression will change and it will get more enthusiastic about its life.

Steve Bowers was a horseman who specialized in driving horses and was well known throughout the horse world as a gentle and effective horseman. He passed his knowledge on to us, his children, Katie and Nathan, who studied next to him for many years. We have taken what we learned from our father, along with lessons from some of the best horsemen in the world, and come up with what we believe is the best way to train a horse.

This book offers many of the key concepts necessary for horsemanship that will result in a happy horse and a happy human. Training a horse takes a lot of patience, as well as understanding. Every interaction has repercussions that can affect the rest of the horse's life. Make sure that everything you do with your horses is relationship based. Be alert, smart, and slow. Remember that Rome wasn't built in a day, and you will not develop the relationship you desire with your horse in a day. Working with a horse takes time and effort, but when all is said and done, it is definitely worth it.

Basic horse knowledge is necessary to make your interactions with the horse both productive and safe. By basic knowledge, we mean remembering what it is that makes a horse a horse. Horses have survived many years on their own by sticking together in herds, fleeing when scared, obeying their instincts, and following their leaders.

When you first approach a horse, it is important to remember that horses are prey animals. In the animal kingdom, all animals are either predators or prey. Predators are born with a natural drive and instinct to hunt and to seek out food in the form of other animals or raw meat. Predators are characterized by eyes set in the front of their heads and not on the sides. A few modern-day predators are dogs, cats, lions, bears, foxes, and wolves. Prey are born with a natural fear of predators and of being hunted and eaten. Prey have eyes set to the outside of their heads, making it easier for them to see what is coming up behind them. Some modern-day prey animals are rabbits, deer, horses, and cows. We humans are the top predators, and horses are extreme prey animals, so we naturally do not have the same instincts or drives. What motivates me does not necessarily motivate my horse. Horses are also born with different levels of instinct. Some horses have a lot of prey and self-preservation instinct, whereas others have very little. People get along with horses that do not have much prey or self-preservation instinct. These attributes are specific to each individual horse and not specific to breeds.

Historically, this is the view most horses had every day. Cattle are no longer a major part of daily training; however, they are a nice way of giving your horse a job. Horses really come to life when they push a cow, and you may be surprised at what sort of response you get from the horse when you work it with cattle. The cattle can also be very useful in getting a horse over its fear of deer and other wildlife.

People tend to have a relatively easy time training dogs because they are predators and are motivated by the same things that motivate humans. Horses, being prey animals, develop relationships with humans only with learning and understanding on the part of humans. Due to their status as prey animals, when left alone, horses will protect themselves blindly, which means they will have no regard for personal pain or death when faced with something that is scaring or attacking them. Although they have been domesticated, horses are still prey animals. The most well-trained animals in the world still have natural instincts. It is important to understand these things so that you can work with horses' instincts and not against them.

As you are training your horse, make sure you are not trying to make the horse into something it is not. A lot of people try to turn their horses into motorcycles, go-carts, or four-wheelers and then do not understand why the horses do not like to be caught, saddled, or ridden. If you just want to get on a horse, run out the lane, and run back in, you would be better off buying a

It is important to think about your center of gravity in reference to your horse's center of gravity when you are jumping your horse. When you look at the side view, you notice that the rider's center of gravity is in line with the horse's center of gravity. If you were to draw a line between both centers of gravity, they would make a straight line to the ground.

You should not quit desensitizing your horse when you get onto its back. It is important to stay relaxed and play with things on the horse's back. Here, the trainer is twirling a rope and gently laying it onto the horse to get it used to the sight, sound, and feel of the trainer moving the rope on its back.

When you are training, do not take anything that the horse does personally, and as soon as the horse says it is sorry for what it has done, forgive it and move on. There is no room for grudges in horse training.

motorcycle, because what you are doing is in no way related to the horse. The more you can remember and consider these facts, the better you and your horse will get along.

There are dominant horses within every herd. These horses are the leaders of the group. There are others in the herd that are passive and submissive. These horses follow their trusted leader. All the horses come together in the herd to make up a hierarchy. The more submissive the horse, the lower in the hierarchy it will be. The more aggressive and willful horses will take more dominant roles within the herd.

Safety is a very important aspect of training horses and should never be put by

As you build your relationship with your horse, you will start to notice that when your horse sees you, it will run to get you and bring along all of its friends. This is a horse's herd instinct and its desire to lead its herd to its leader, which makes the human the leader of the entire herd.

the wayside. If you think you can perform a feat with your horse, you are probably right. But keep in mind that you are including in this scenario another living being that looks at things and thinks about them in a completely different way than you do. You need to look at both yourself and your horse when determining whether something should be attempted. All our training exercises will take you through different things you can do with your horse, but make sure to keep a specific emphasis on safety. As you are training your horse, it is going to start to see you as a partner and a leader. But it will take a bit of time to build up the trust, rapport, and respect that we all desire from our horses. Use a lot of caution and stay light on your toes as you are building your relationship. As the relationship grows, you can start to trust the horse more and more.

Make sure to completely read each part of the exercise before attempting it with your horse. If you are unsure of whether or not your horse is doing the exercise correctly, feel free to ask a friend or trusted horseman or -woman about what you are doing. Chances are, after watching you for a few minutes, the horse expert will be able to tell you if you are

As you develop your relationship with your horse, you can do many high-level things such as driving. Driving is the most dangerous thing you could possibly do with a horse. We are solidly attaching two prey animals to the front of a steel blade that mows grass. This takes a strong relationship between the horses and the human for the horses to not be afraid.

Anything that your horse may have fear of can easily be overcome with patience and relaxation. This horse did not want to go through this water. The trainer simply stuck with it, allowed the horse to be fearful for a bit, and the horse walked right in. It is important to not push the horse through its fear. Respect the horse's fear and allow it to think. This will help you create a horse that is level-headed and easy to train.

correctly completing the exercise and if the desired outcome is being achieved.

A very important element of safety is learning to read your horse and knowing when it is agitated, happy, or frustrated. Your horse's behavior will key you in to what is going on with it mentally. When you are trying to read your horse, the best place to look is its face. You can tell a lot about the emotional state of your horse by its ears, eyes, mouth, nose, and breathing. As a horse becomes nervous, its body tightens, its respiration becomes shallow and fast, and its mouth and nose region tightens. The ears will typically lock and no longer rotate around and listen to its surroundings. A horse's eyes are connected to its ears, so if both ears are pointed forward, that is where both eyes are pointed. The ears may also become completely pinned down toward the rear.

When your horse is completely relaxed, look for slow, deep breathing mixed with a few sighs. Also watch for a cocked rear leg. A relaxed horse will lick its lips. The head position of a relaxed horse is a natural extension of its back. Try to have your horse relaxed, calm, and cool at the end of each training session. If you need to stop and spend some quiet, quality time with the horse after each training session, that is okay. Make sure your horse exhibits the above characteristics before the end of the training session. It is not healthy to put the horse back in its paddock while it is in an agitated state. Your horse will mostly remember how it felt after, not during, your training session. It may take you a while to be able to truly read your horse—the same way it takes a mechanic a long time to know when a motor does not sound right. If you pay close attention to your horse, you will be able to tell when it is off, even just slightly, even when other people cannot tell anything is wrong. This is the beauty of a relationship-based training program. You and the horse know each other.

There are quite a few different sports in the horse world. We encourage you to follow your sporting dreams, just as long as the dreams do not get in the way of your relationship with your horse. We want you to put the relationship with the horse first. The sport and the desire to win should come second.

Parts of a Horse

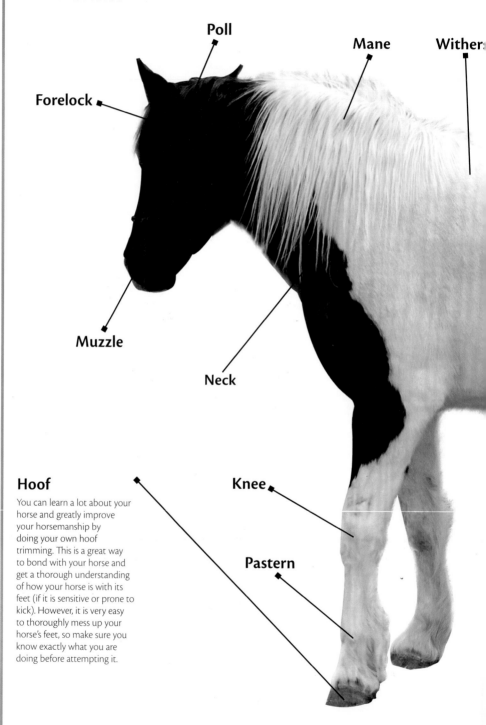

Poll

Mane

Withers

Forelock

Muzzle

Neck

Hoof

You can learn a lot about your
horse and greatly improve
your horsemanship by
doing your own hoof
trimming. This is a great way
to bond with your horse and
get a thorough understanding
of how your horse is with its
feet (if it is sensitive or prone to
kick). However, it is very easy
to thoroughly mess up your
horse's feet, so make sure you
know exactly what you are
doing before attempting it.

Knee

Pastern

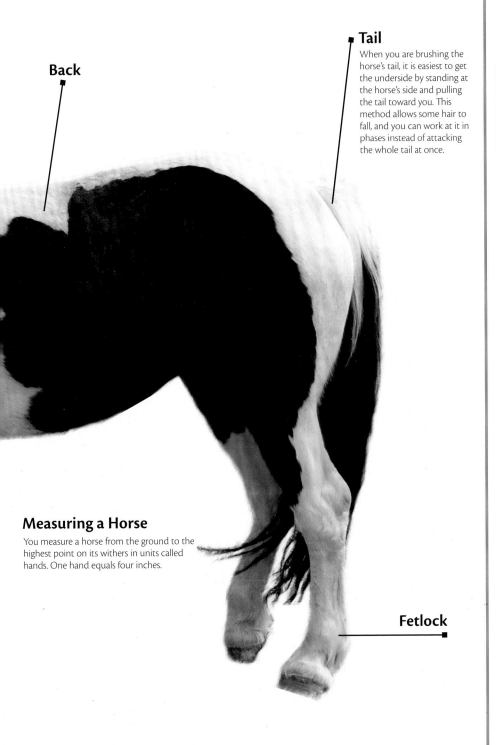

Back

Tail

When you are brushing the horse's tail, it is easiest to get the underside by standing at the horse's side and pulling the tail toward you. This method allows some hair to fall, and you can work at it in phases instead of attacking the whole tail at once.

Measuring a Horse

You measure a horse from the ground to the highest point on its withers in units called hands. One hand equals four inches.

Fetlock

SELECTING AND CARING FOR YOUR HORSE

When selecting a horse for purchase, it is important to look at the activities you want to do with the horse. Decide exactly what goals you have for both yourself and your horse. Do you want to compete? Is trail riding your dream? Are you going to be working with cattle? Does driving interest you? Or is this horse going to be one that does a little bit of everything? If you are going to be working with cattle, it is not a great idea to buy a Belgian. If you are going to be plowing fields, you probably do not want to buy an Arabian. An Arabian can pull a plow, and a Belgian can work with cattle, but certain breeds of horses are made to excel at certain things. It is best to select and purchase a horse that is bred to keep up with you and your horsemanship dreams. There are certain traits and attributes that make each breed special. It is a good idea to research breeds that interest you to get a better idea of what each horse was bred and made to do. The horse you purchase will not be exactly like the breed description, but it will most likely be a close match, and the description should give you a good starting point in selecting the perfect horse.

When buying a horse, you must also consider your skill level, as well as your desire to train. If you are not interested in training your own horse and want a sweet old plug that will never get you into any trouble and does not need much education, then you should probably not buy a young colt. If you want to start your own horse, it is not a good idea to buy a horse that someone else has already tried and failed to train or that has had less than perfect training results. A clean slate is always the best bet if you want to train your own horse. If you wrote a message on a brand-new chalkboard and then erased it the best you could, you would still be able to read the message. Young horses are like clean slates. If you write on them, mess up, and try to erase what was written, the original message will still be there, even if it is very faint, no matter how well you try to erase it. It is best to do the original writing on the slate correctly.

There is nothing like the feeling of riding a classy, well-trained horse such as this one. But can you ride this horse to its fullest potential? If you are going to ride an athlete, you need to be an athlete yourself. If you buy a horse that is at level ten as far as its athleticism and training, and you are only at level one as far as your athleticism and abilities, then the two of you together will be at level one. You are only as strong as your weakest partner.

A young horse may be a little scary at first, but they are good for your training. They will present a lot of different problems, which will give you an opportunity to learn. But compared to an older horse, the problems of a young horse are easier to fix, because they have not been problems for very long. Remember the chalkboard analogy—you want a clean slate.

That way, you are not fighting to erase or cover up something that has happened in your horse's past.

The last determining factor in selecting a horse is the price. There are many nice horses out there. The opposite is also true; there are a lot of really bad horses out there. It is important to be extremely cautious when selecting your horse to make sure you get one of the nice ones. Just because a horse costs more does not mean it will ride better than a cheap horse. It is also important not to cheap out and buy a horse that will waste

> If you want to start your own horse, it is not a good idea to buy a horse that someone else has already tried and failed to train or that has had less than perfect training results. A clean slate is always the best bet if you want to train your own horse.

your time and money. The price on a horse is simply the initiation fee; they all cost the same once you own them. We always tell people who are considering a horse to ask themselves, "Can I afford to lose this horse if it dies tomorrow?" If the answer is that losing the horse would hurt but not break your bank, and that you would be able to continue with your horse world dreams, then I would say the horse is within your price range. But if you look at a horse and say, "Boy, if I lost that horse, I would be broke," that horse is out of your price range. Horses are living animals, so it is a real possibility that they could die at any point. It is a good idea to plan for the worst both emotionally and financially. This advice may seem harsh, but it is the reality of life.

Once you have decided on the type of horse you wish to buy, along with the amount of money you are willing to spend, you are free to start looking for your horse. Some people prefer buying privately rather than at an auction. Just know that you can get yourself into trouble either way. There is a popular sedative drug on the market that is commonly known as ace. This drug is illegal to use in horse sales, and it is often hard to prove that it has been used. I have witnessed aced horses being sold at auctions, and I have also encountered them in private sales. The best way to tell if a horse has been aced without doing a blood test is to have the person selling the horse ride it clear through all three gears: from walk and trot to canter. An aced horse will have an impossibly hard time trying to canter. It will be quite obvious to you that the horse does not look normal or healthy. Even older horses should be able to move through all three gears, so do not allow the person selling the horse to give you any excuses for why the horse cannot canter. Ace is a depressant and will make the horse slow to react. It will want to stay in one place and sleep. Another way to avoid purchasing an aced horse is to buy from someone you trust who has a good reputation. People do not seem to have a hard time lying to strangers, but they will generally be honest with a friend.

Local newspapers often advertise horses for sale. Various online resources are also available. Once you pick out a horse, it is important that you be very thorough and scrutinize every little detail when you look at it. I also make sure that the person selling the horse shows me everything he or she says the horse can do. If I were looking at a horse that was advertised as a good driving horse, I would not believe it was a good driving horse until I watched the owner drive it. If you arrive and the horse is already out and saddled, it is not a good sign. The horse

Be wary of the horse that does not know how to respond to rein pressure. You can fix a problem like this, although it can be difficult if you are not sure of what you are doing. It is best to avoid horses that look like this unless you are skilled enough to help them get over the problem.

Before you purchase a horse, try to see it in as many situations as possible. If the horse is being sold as well broken to ride, make sure you see it ride a lot. You'll want to see it more than just one time in its pen. When you are watching a seller ride a horse, think of places you would like to see him or her ride the horse. If you can push both the human and horse out of their comfort zones, you will get a better idea of what it is you are looking at.

may have problems being caught or saddled. Or the owner may have worked the horse down and made it look nice right before your arrival. When it comes to spending your hard-earned money, you should take no one at his or her word. Seeing is believing.

When I first arrive at an auction or stable to look at a horse, I stand back and watch the owner with the horse. You do not want to immediately jump in and start working with the horse. Make sure you closely scrutinize every detail, from the way the horse catches to how it leads. How is the horse to saddle, and how it is to mount and ride? Never let the owner ride in only an arena and take his or her word that the horse rides well outside a fenced area. Have the owner ride out the lane and up the road. Watch the horse's reactions to the different things it encounters. I never ride a horse that the owner has not ridden first. After it is quite clear that the horse is safe to ride and after the owner has done a few different things with it, you can ride the horse. Watching a horse with its current owner is the best way to learn about a horse. When you first mount a horse and try it out, it will not look or respond the same way it did when the owner was riding it. Do not worry about this—the horse is not used to you, and you are not used to the horse. Give yourself some time to really get the feel of the horse and let the horse get the feel of you. It is not bad if the horse you are looking at is not the right horse for you. There are a lot of horses out there, and too many people buy a horse simply because it was the first one they looked at.

Here are some other important things to watch for when looking at a horse. How is the horse with its feet? Does it pick them up gently and hold them up, or does the horse try to pull its foot away from you and keep it on the ground? How does the horse take a bridle? Does it throw its head in the air when the bit is inserted in its mouth? Does the horse have a verifiable age? To verify the age and physical health of the horse, you may want to have a veterinarian perform a pre-purchase exam. A vet's knowledge and expertise is well worth the cost of a pre-purchase exam. We will not go into depth on all the things that could be physically wrong with a horse, since the list is so long. We mostly want to focus on the mental and emotional well-being of the horse and whether or not the horse fits you on an emotional, physical, and mental level.

Before you purchase the perfect horse, make sure you are able to appropriately care for it. Horses need four primary things to survive: food, water, shelter, and space. These things are the core of what every animal needs to survive, besides the obvious oxygen component. If you cannot provide these four things for your horse, it will not be able to live. Before you commit to the ownership of a horse, it is important to think about the responsibility it takes to care for it. You are putting the horse into captivity, which means you are taking away its power to take care of itself. You are taking on the responsibility of providing food, water, shelter, and space. You need to be able to feed the horse daily. You also need to make sure the horse always has fresh water. The horse will also need shelter from storms and sun. If you are going to modify your horse's coat by giving it a show clip body clip, or by docking its tail, you need to plan on blanketing it. It is your responsibility to make sure that the horse does not freeze to death. Space is the hardest thing for people to provide. Keeping a horse in a box stall is a cheap and easy method of sheltering a horse. However, it is extremely detrimental to the emotional, mental, and physical well-being of the horse. If you are going to keep your horse in a box stall, be sure you can get it out every day and allow it space to move its feet. If you keep your horse in a box stall full-time, you have to clean the stall every day. If you do

When you pick up a horse's hoof, you should be able to do it without hurting your back. Once you have the hoof up, you should be able to hold it without the horse trying to slam it back onto the ground. Be wary of horses of whose feet you cannot pick up. This may be evidence of a larger problem.

not, there will be a buildup of ammonia, and you run the risk of damaging your horse's lungs. You cannot deny your horse any one of the four critical elements of life. You will permanently damage the horse and would have been better off not purchasing the horse in the first place. If you do not provide all these elements for your horse, you are guilty of animal abuse.

People often do not feed their horses properly for the jobs the horses are going to perform. If your horse is not going to be doing a lot of physical labor, such as plowing

or running long distances, you do not need to feed it as much as a horse that will be working hard. Many people feed one horse more than I would feed a team of horses that had been plowing fields all day long. If your horse has a sedentary or slow lifestyle, it should be fed appropriately to avoid physical problems associated with being overweight, such as diabetes, founder, laminitis, and navicular syndrome.

Diabetes is a common problem for horses that eat too much and don't get enough exercise. When it is not moving enough, a

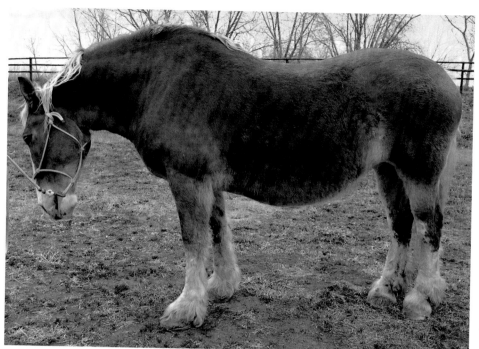

As you can see, obesity hurts a horse's back in addition to its legs and feet. Obesity has prematurely aged this horse's back and ruined its knees. Its coffin bone is trying to push through the sole of its foot. People believe they are being nice by giving a horse a little extra food. In actuality, they are being negligent and abusing the animal by throwing it off its diet.

horse will store the unused energy it takes in as fat. Fat deposits are the result of the horse's inability to process food appropriately and regulate insulin levels as it should. This condition is very similar to adult onset (type 2) diabetes. This type of diabetes in humans can be regulated with a healthier diet and more exercise. The same is true for horses, although diabetic horses are hard to get moving due to their excess weight. Some complications can occur with equine diabetes, including laminitis and founder.

Laminitis and founder are painful inflammations of a horse's feet. Laminitis is generally found in front feet but can affect hind feet as well. The tissue damage and complications from attacks of laminitis are what we call founder. If this condition goes untreated, the laminae, the layer between the coffin bone and the hoof wall, can be damaged. If this connection breaks down, the coffin bone can eventually push through the horse's sole and into the ground. Laminitis and founder are both caused by eating too much food in large quantities.

Another problem that can occur in a horse's foot is navicular syndrome, which occurs when the navicular bone becomes inflamed. The navicular bone is surrounded by bursae, or bags of fluid that help lubricate the joint. When bones in the horse's foot have too much pressure on them, they can begin to harden and not receive enough blood flow. They can also begin to cramp the bursae, keeping them from preventing pain during movement.

Horses need four primary things to survive: food, water, shelter, and space.

There is nothing better than good, old-fashioned grass hay. It is available at most feed stores.

All of the above-mentioned diseases and health problems can be prevented by keeping your horse on the appropriate diet for its lifestyle. You may notice changes in your horse as it ages; take these changes into account as you continually review your horse's feeding plan and diet. Make sure you are also looking at how much the horse moves on a daily basis. All these factors play into whether or not to modify your horse's feeding.

We advise people in most areas to feed only grass hay during the summer and winter months. Winter can be cold and may require a hotter feed to keep a horse's weight up. Grass hay is easy on a horse's digestive system and is not too high octane for the average horse's lifestyle. A lot of people do not get along with their horses simply because the horses are overfed. If you feed a horse a high-calorie, high-energy feed and then expect it to stand still without burning off

that energy, you will be thoroughly frustrated. It is essentially like loading kids up on soda pop and sugar and then taking them to the movies and expecting them to sit still and be quiet. If you give those same kids water and a low-sugar diet, they will be much less fidgety, dysfunctional, and annoying. The same thing goes for a horse. The appropriate amount of feed for each horse is different, depending on the horse's size, age, workload, and metabolism. A young horse that gets worked one day a week does not need to be eating alfalfa or grain. These foods are full of too much energy and too many calories. If that same horse is working six to eight hours a day in the fields or on the roads, it will need a high-calorie feed such as alfalfa or grain. Always think about the rate of energy use compared to the rate of energy intake. If the rate of energy use is greater than the rate of energy intake, the horse will be tired, lose

continued on page 31

What if . . . my horse is bad about picking up its feet?

If your horse is bad about picking up its feet, take it into an open area to do this exercise safely. When working on a horse's feet, especially a horse that doesn't like to pick up its feet, it is a good idea to have another person around to help you, in case you get into trouble. Remember to always start on the front feet and move to the rear.

Go to the left side of the horse, take the end of your lead rope, and run it between the horse's front legs. (It is a good idea to have a long rope for this exercise.) You will have just created a loop that runs down, around the horse's left front leg, and back up to your hand. Lower the loop from up high on the horse's leg to just below the fetlock. Put both parts of the rope into your left hand. Slowly add pressure and lift the foot straight up. Pull with steady pressure until you feel the horse shift its weight off the foot you are asking it to lift.

As soon as you feel the horse shift its weight, release the pressure and start again. As soon as your horse relaxes with its foot raised, gently set it back down on the toe.

The most important part of this exercise is that you get the horse to set its foot down on the toe. This is the ultimate sign of relaxation and that the horse is putting no weight on that particular leg.

All the problems with horses being bad about their feet can be fixed by always setting the horse's foot back down on the toe. Continue doing this exercise with the rope until the horse lifts up its foot when you gently apply pressure.

A lot of time and patience are key to making this exercise work. If you pick up the horse's foot and the horse thrashes the foot back and forth, stay out of the way of the moving foot, but do not release it unless you have to. If the foot becomes too much for you to handle and the horse gets it back onto the ground, start over and pick up the foot again. After thrashing its foot back and forth, the horse will eventually relax.

continued on page 28

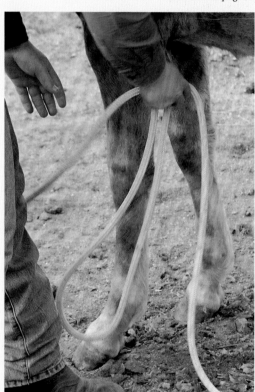

As you pass your rope between the horse's legs, watch for any signs of agitation on its face. The horse may not particularly enjoy the feel of a rope between its front legs, and you run the risk of the horse pawing or striking out at you. The more attention you can pay to the horse, the safer you will be.

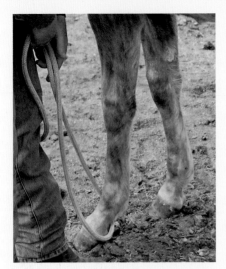 

Before you begin applying pressure to lift the foot, lower and raise your rope a few times along the horse's leg, so it gets used to the feel of your rope. This may be the first time your horse has ever had something around its leg. The good thing about using your rope to stroke the horse's leg is that you do not have to use your hand at first. This increases your safety and lowers the likelihood of you getting hurt.

If your horse thrashes its foot back and forth, make sure to keep your knees back, so you don't get whacked with a hoof. Some large horses are strong and heavy enough to push you down and underneath their feet. If you think that is going to happen, let go and start again.

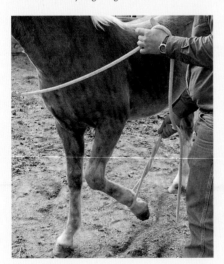 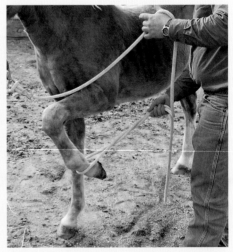

Once you have lifted the horse's foot and it has stopped thrashing it around, slowly lower it down and onto the toe. Even as you are lowering the hoof onto the toe, pay close attention to what the horse is thinking, so you can be ready if it does something unexpected.

As you are lowering the foot, the horse will likely go back to thrashing it back and forth. Be patient and persistent, pick the hoof back up, and hold it until the horse relaxes again. Once you feel the horse relax, again lower the foot onto the toe. Remember to keep your knees and feet out of the way of a thrashing foot, so that you don't get hurt.

This is what the hoof should look like when you finally release it. Once the hoof is gently set on the toe, completely release all pressure and remove your rope from around the horse's leg. Your horse may rest the foot on its toe for only a few seconds or for a while. As long as the hoof is resting on the toe, pet the horse and do not pick up any more feet.

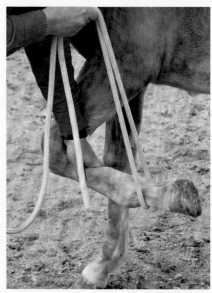

Notice that the trainer does not have to bend over to pick up the horse's hoof. This can be a real back saver. The rope also increases your safety by keeping you a bit farther from the action. This is a good trick to use on horses that are bad about their feet, as well as on older horses that are fine about their feet.

When you go to set the hoof back down on the toe, the horse may stomp the foot on the ground itself. Let the foot down slowly and gently. If the horse begins to thrash it back and forth as you are lowering the foot, lift it back up. Hold the foot up until the horse stops moving and relaxes. Start lowering it again. Continue doing this until the horse will let you lower the foot all the way to the ground. You should be able to set the hoof on its toe without the horse taking it from you or stomping it on the ground.

Once both front feet are easy to pick up with the rope, do the same exercise with the back feet. The difference between the front and back feet is that with the back feet, you want to stay toward the front of the horse and pull the foot forward instead of pulling it toward the rear.

Make sure the rope is not wrapped around your hands and that you are in front of the horse's foot to avoid getting kicked. Most horses initially kick when they feel a back foot being picked up. If your horse does kick out, the rope will pop out of your hand, and you can start over.

As with the front feet, get the horse to lift up its foot gently and set it back down on the toe. Patience is a virtue, and it must be exercised during this project. Pick up all four feet until the horse gently shifts its weight and picks up its foot with light pressure from the rope. Using a rope to pick up the feet is much gentler on your back and much safer than the alternative method of bending over, picking up a foot with your hand, and getting your face next to the horse.

continued on page 30

29

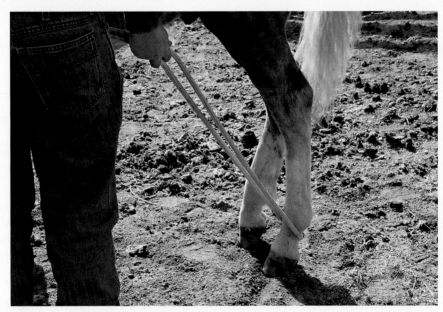

Once you have placed your rope around the horse's leg, gently apply pressure. As you can see in this photo, when the horse felt pressure on its leg, it shifted its weight onto that foot, pushing its weight and leg farther into the ground. Continue holding the pressure until the horse shifts off that foot.

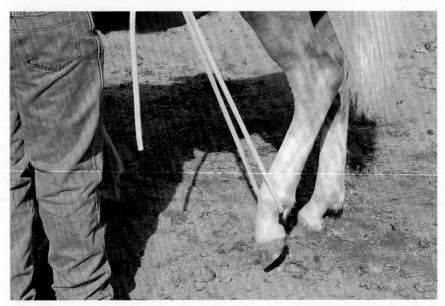

This is what the rear hoof should look like as you are setting it onto its toe. Make sure you stay with the horse if it decides it does not want to set its hoof on the toe. Continue holding the foot up until you are able to get the horse to gently lower it onto the toe. Stay forward and to the side so that you do not get kicked.

continued from page 26

weight, possibly get sick, and slowly die. If the rate of energy intake is greater than the rate of use, the horse will gain weight and have high energy. Your goal should be to find a feed that equalizes the rate of energy intake and the rate of energy use. If you feed your horse the appropriate feed, then its feet, legs, hair, teeth, and mind will all be healthy.

Now that nutrition has been appropriately addressed, let's look at another aspect of horse care: the horse's feet. Horses are unique in that they naturally trim their feet when left alone. To trim their hooves, horses need two things. First, the soil must be rocky so that as it walks around, the rocks slowly break and chip its hooves. Second, the horse must move around. If the horse does not need or want to move around, its feet will constantly grow and never trim themselves. The only problem with horses trimming their own feet is that they don't look as nice as professionally trimmed feet.

A lot of people believe a horse should always wear shoes, while others think a horse should never wear shoes. True horsemen will tell you that neither of these schools of thought is correct. The activities your horse is going to be doing will determine whether or not it needs shoes. The main thing to think about is the rate of wear versus the rate of growth. Imagine you were asked to run a mile barefoot on concrete. Once you got to the end of the mile, your feet would be sore and torn up. This is because your rate of wear exceeded your rate of growth. The skin on the bottom of your feet regenerates itself, but not fast enough for running barefoot over long distances. You end up wearing your feet out, which is very painful. The same idea applies to a horse. If the horse is moving on roads or rocky terrain for long distances, its feet won't be able to keep up with the wear. The horse may be fine barefoot for a day, but it will not be able to endure high rates of

wear over a long period. Therefore, the horse needs shoes. On the other hand, if I told you to sit in your house with your running shoes on all day long, your feet would eventually feel uncomfortable, and they would change form from being so restricted. If there is no real wear or only slight wear on your horse's hooves, there is no need to put shoes on your horse. Just as wearing running shoes all day long and not doing anything would change the shape of your feet over time, wearing shoes all the time will constrict the horse's heels and totally reshape the feet. Shoeing your horse can be used to your benefit if the horse's hooves need reshaping. A good farrier can use a shoe as a tool to reshape the foot, so that the horse can eventually safely and comfortably go barefoot.

Whether your horse is wearing shoes or not, the rate of growth will eventually exceed the rate of wear, and you will need to trim the horse's feet. If the horse is wearing shoes, the shoes will need to be reset. You can learn a lot about your horse and greatly improve your horsemanship by doing your own hoof trimming. This is a great way to bond with your horse and get a thorough understanding of how your horse is with its feet (if it is sensitive or prone to kick) and how your farrier feels about trimming or shoeing your horse. However, it is very easy to thoroughly mess up your horse's feet, so make sure you know exactly what you are doing before attempting to trim horses' feet or reset their shoes. If you are going to trim your horse's feet, it's important to find further resources to continue your education on this process. It is not as easy as it looks, so do not just go and try it. There is an old saying in the farrier world that goes, "No foot, no horse." This means that the nicest horse in the world would be absolutely useless if you ruined its feet. So be very careful when dealing with your horse's feet.

continued on page 38

What if . . . my horse is extremely bad or dangerous about its hind feet?

It is common to run into horses that are incredibly bad about their hind feet in that they don't like their feet being touched and are prone to kick. There is only one way to get a horse over this issue safely. Take the horse into a round or square pen with a tall fence. Have another person go outside the fence. Pass the rope through a high rail to the person on the

To get your rope secured around the horse's back leg, enlarge your loop and then back the horse into the loop. Your partner on the other side of the fence will be the one to actually back up the horse. Communication is key.

As soon as you have the loop around the horse's leg, rub the rope up and down, so the horse can get used to the feel.

outside. This person has the job of keeping the horse's nose at that particular spot on the fence.

The person outside the fence must also be relational at the appropriate time and give in to the horse if it becomes too overwhelmed by what you are doing. Make sure to use a long rope and tell your assistant not to allow the horse to drag him or her through the fence or bang his or her hands against the rails.

The assistant should stand 1 foot away from the fence to accomplish these requirements and keep safe.

Next, take a rope approximately 20 feet or more in length. Tie a bowline (see page 36) into the end of the rope and run the rope through the loop. Once you have tied your knot and looped the rope into it, the rope should look like a lasso.

Open the loop until it is large and place it over the horse's hock to the rear, so that if the horse takes a step backward, it will step into the loop. This will make a loop around the leg that will be soft on the leg and release when you set the horse's foot back down.

continued on page 34

33

We do not want to use the end of the rope that has a snap on it and then snap it back onto itself, because it is too hard and could possibly hurt the horse's leg. Lower the loop, place it below the fetlock, and take up the slack.

Walk away from the horse while keeping the slack out of the rope but not pulling on the horse's foot. Go to the end of the rope straight behind the horse and gently ask the horse to lift its foot by pulling on the rope. As soon as the horse gives just a little bit or shifts its weight off that foot, release the pressure and give the horse a moment to think.

Pull up on the horse's foot again and raise it off the ground into approximately the position

it would be in if you were trimming or shoeing the foot. At this point, a lot of horses will have some form of fit or tantrum, which typically takes the form of kicking at you and the rope. This is where your assistant helps by keeping the horse's front end in place. Hold your tension as the horse kicks at the rope and tries to get rid of the pressure. Do your best to stay with it until the horse stops moving and relaxes. As soon as the horse stops kicking, release the tension on the foot and let the horse have its foot back. Then lift the foot up again.

Continue doing this exercise until you can gently pull on the rope and have the horse shift its

The beauty of teaching your horse to pick up its hind feet this way is that you can stay far enough away to not get kicked in the teeth. Notice how the back person is able to pull the foot up to the exact place it would be if it were being trimmed.

As soon as your horse has relaxed, gently set the hoof down onto the toe and release pressure. You are now going to do this exercise just as you did with just one person pulling the hoof forward.

weight off the hoof. Then you can pull again and get the horse to lift its foot gently without kicking at you.

The ultimate goal is to get the horse to set its foot down onto its toe. Once the horse is good with the left foot, move to the right foot. Be careful removing your rope. Continue doing this exercise until your horse safely and easily lifts both hind feet.

If your horse has had a lot of years of being a troublemaker with its feet, it may take you a few sessions to achieve the desired outcome. Since your horse may be kicking at the rope, you will want to wear gloves to protect your hands from rope burn.

continued on page 36

How to tie a Bowline knot

To tie a bowline knot, begin by creating a loop on the standing part of the rope. Place the loop in your right hand and the tail of the rope in your left.

Run the tail of the rope through the loop around the standing part of the rope and back through the same loop you just came through.

The loop in the end of your rope will make your rope into an oversized lariat. It will be soft on your horse's leg, and you do not have to worry about hurting the horse as you would if you used an actual lariat or snapped your rope back onto itself.

This is what a finished bowline looks like. You have just created a loop in the end of your rope. The bowline knot is very useful in many situations and is actually stronger than the rope itself.

Grooming

Many people get too caught up on grooming. Grooming has nothing to do with the mind of the horse and everything to do with how it looks on the outside. People get tricked into buying a mentally poor horse because it is well groomed. Often, a horse is well groomed because that is all its owners can do with it.

Remember that pretty is as pretty does.

A certain amount of grooming is necessary for safety. You do not want to be riding around on top of a muddy horse or one that has burrs and dirt underneath the saddle pad. An easy way to clean your horse is to currycomb its entire body and brush it with a soft brush before you ride. Another easy way

What if . . . my horse is afraid of being washed?

If your horse is afraid of being washed, take it into a round pen with a water faucet. Attach a long hose with a trigger nozzle to the water faucet.

The hardest part of this exercise is keeping yourself and your horse from getting tangled up in the hose, so make sure you have enough hose and it is pulled far enough into the pen.

Start on the left side, standing at the horse's shoulder, approximately 2 feet away from the horse. Hold the hose with your right hand and the lead rope with your left. You are about to make the round pen a bit muddy, so be sure to wear the appropriate footwear.

Squeeze the trigger on the nozzle and allow a steady stream of water to pour straight out, parallel to the horse. The stream of water should not hit the horse.

If your horse starts to move, continue spraying and try to keep the spray parallel to the horse. With the other hand, keep the horse's head with you, so that the horse pivots around its front feet.

As soon as the horse stops its feet, stop spraying the water. Pet the horse, tell it how smart it is, and then begin again.

Continue this exercise until you can turn the hose on and off without the horse moving

its feet. Once your horse is good about that, start the spray parallel to its body and spray the water on the left hind foot and leg region. Odds are, the horse will begin to pivot again. Do the same exercise as before; keep the spray flowing onto its leg until the horse stops its feet.

It is important not to let the horse run around you as it tries to get away from the spray. If it does, it will take many hours for the horse to stop. Keep the front end with you and keep the horse pivoting around its front feet. Once the horse stops, turn off the hose, pet the horse, and tell it how smart it is. Continue this process and slowly spray your way to the front of the horse. Each time you reach a spot where the horse wants to move, allow it to move by pivoting around the front feet. Continue with your spray until the horse stops its feet.

As soon as the horse stops its feet while being sprayed, immediately stop the flow of water. If you do this with the correct timing, the horse will quickly learn to stop its feet when it feels the water.

On a small scale, you are teaching your horse to be safe when being washed. But on a larger scale, you are building a response to fear into your horse—to stop its feet when it is scared.

to clean your horse is to wash it. Washing will remove all the dust, dirt, and mud.

It is never nice to see a horse with witches knots in its mane or tail, so keep a close eye out for tangles. A witches knot is the equivalent of a dreadlock. If your horse has witches knots in its mane or tail, a nice detangler is WD-40. Spray a small amount onto the horse's mane or tail and gently brush the knot out. With the detangler, you won't rip or tear out as much hair as you would without it. When you are brushing the horse's tail, it is easiest to get the underside by standing at the horse's side and pulling the tail toward you. This method allows some hair to fall, and you can work at it in sections instead of attacking the whole tail at once.

Another important element of grooming is keeping flies off your horse, especially if you live in a warm climate where bugs and flies thrive. Flies can be very distracting to your horse. If you have ever had a frustrating itch that you cannot quite reach, then you know what a horse feels like when flies congregate in a spot it can't quite get to. This situation can cause a horse to nearly panic as it tries to get the flies off its back or face. In some places, it is common to see horses running around like crazy at night, trying to get rid of flies or mosquitoes biting at their flesh. Spray your horse down with an organic fly repellant whenever needed. Marigold and citronella spray work well. Use a natural, organic fly spray, because humans and horses absorb substances through their skin. You would not want your horse drinking most fly repellants, because the poison would get into the horse's system. So don't spray your horse down with that same poison, because it will be absorbed through the horse's skin.

When you are brushing the horse's tail, it is easiest to get the underside by standing at the horse's side and pulling the tail toward you.

Horse Health

The horse world is definitely split in its feelings about veterinarians. I have found that people tend to view the vet much like they view their own doctor. Some people take their animals to the vet, and themselves to the doctor, on a regular schedule to ensure good health. Other people see the doctor and the vet only when something is wrong and they need assistance. Neither approach is right or wrong in my book; it is a personal preference. Use your own discretion as to what is best for you and your horse.

FIRST IMPRESSIONS

With horses, first impressions are very important. The impression you give your horse is going to affect how it rides. You make your first impression when you approach your horse to catch it. The way you catch your horse can give it many different messages. You can give the horse the impression that you are scared of it, that it is the boss and that you have no confidence. Or you can give the

The horse is engaging with the trainer in this photo. The horse is intently looking at the trainer, saying, "What are you going to do?" As you build your relationship with your horse, you will receive the same questioning gaze. It is a very positive experience to have your horse looking at you this way.

As the trainer went in to catch the horse, the horse decided it did not want anything to do with the trainer. The horse broke off from the trainer and tried to get away, looking for an exit.

impression that you are the owner of the situation, are not scared, are the boss, and are full of confidence.

When you approach your horse, make sure you approach it with confidence and in a relaxed manner. If you have been around horses for a long time, you have probably seen someone sneaking up on a horse. The person hides the halter and lead rope behind his or her back and slowly edges up to the horse with a hand out, saying, "Easy, boy. Easy." Horses are not incapable of realizing what you are doing. They realize that by walking up to them like this, you are going to do something to them. Their focus is on trying to discover what is hidden behind the sneaky human's back. Make sure that when you walk to your horse, you do it with confidence. Keep the halter and lead rope at your side or in front of you, in plain

view. Even if you expect your horse to walk away, walk up to it with the attitude that you expect it to stay where it is. This approach will encourage the horse to stand still. If your horse does walk away from you, do not sneak up to catch it. It is better for the horse to walk away from you with the halter and lead rope in plain view than to sneak up to the horse and, as a result, have the horse not trust you.

A horse that is hard to catch is the result of a much bigger problem. The horse does not trust you or want to be near you; it would rather get away from you. It is important to realize that this is a relationship problem. As trainers, we want to make sure that we are always fighting the disease and not the symptom. The symptom, in this case, is a horse that is hard to catch. The disease is that the horse does not trust you. *continued on page 48*

What if . . . my horse does not like to be caught?

If your horse does not like to be caught, the worst thing you can do is catch it. You want to have quality time with your horse, with no agenda other than having friendly time together.

After spending a lot of quality time petting and loving your horse, you are ready to catch it. But remember not to revert to sneaking up on the horse. This approach may work three or four times, but it does not last in the long run and does nothing but hurt your relationship with the horse.

Walk to the horse boldly but not flamboyantly. As you walk, keep your halter in front of you and in the horse's sight. If the horse walks away, it is okay. As the horse walks away, twirl your rope toward the horse and chase it off. Then go to the middle of whatever circle the horse is running in.

When you go to the center of your horse's pen, it will typically build a big circle around you that runs the border of the fence. Some horses will dart back and forth along one fence row. Do not allow your horse to do this. Encourage the horse to move in a circle by your body placement.

As the horse is leaving, the trainer continues walking toward it. As the trainer walks toward the horse, he twirls the rope at it. Even if the trainer walked forward to catch the horse and it turned away and stopped, the trainer would still chase the horse away. You do not want to catch a horse that is not facing you. This gets the horse out and into the circle traveling around you. Make sure to twirl the rope forward and not backward. You run the risk of accidentally hitting yourself in the face if you twirl it backward.

As the horse travels around the circle, the trainer steps out in front of the horse, with an arm out as if to catch the horse with that hand. As soon as the horse looks at the trainer with both eyes, the trainer stops and backs up.

When the trainer walked backward as the horse was looking at him, the motion encouraged the horse to come in to him. Notice how the horse turned the rest of its body toward the trainer and is going in to greet him.

Stand in the center of the circle even if you are not in the center of the pen. At first, as the horse is going around you, it will pay no attention to you. The horse will have its body tight and angled away from the circle instead of into the circle.

Imagine looking at your horse from above. You want your horse's body to have a curve to it, with the curve pointing to the inside of the circle it is running on. Let the horse go around you until it starts to pay attention to you. You will notice that as the horse begins to pay attention to you, its body will begin to curve to the inside of the circle instead of the outside. As you are doing this, you will quickly realize that it is hard to teach animals or humans anything when they are not paying attention. The point of making the horse move around you is to allow it to reach a place where it can pay attention to and learn from you.

Once your horse has let off some of its steam and starts to notice you—this may be with one ear or two—step out in front of the horse at the

The colt quickly lost interest again, thinking it was better to pursue life away from the trainer.

continued on page 44

43

As the colt was losing its connection with the trainer, the trainer chased it forward. This showed the horse that there is pressure when it goes away from the trainer and the opposite when it stays close.

This colt has a personal bubble that is approximately 2 feet away from its body. The trainer walks into the horse's personal bubble, but not far enough to scare the horse away, and waits for a moment.

After the trainer has spent a moment in the colt's personal bubble, he turns and walks away. Notice that this move immediately made the colt want to be with the trainer. After that, the trainer could not get the horse out of his back pocket.

halfway mark of the circle. Do not step in front of the horse with only a few feet to spare. Doing this will make the horse stop too soon. Make sure you are far enough away that the horse can slow down and think about what you are proposing.

As your horse is coming around, it will eventually be pointed straight at you. When this happens, quickly walk backward, slowly spiraling in on the circle. If you back up straight to the middle of the circle, the turn will be too difficult for the horse, and it will not follow you. Walking backward encourages your horse to come to you. If your horse does come toward you, continue backing up until the horse catches up to you. It is highly unlikely that your horse will come to you on the very first try.

Once you notice that your horse is no longer paying attention to you, go back to the center of

When you halter a horse, always start by walking up, petting it, and laying your lead rope up over its back, so that it stays out of your way and does not get dirty. No one likes holding onto a lead rope covered in horse manure.

continued on page 46

45

Stand facing your horse. Reach over the top of the horse's neck with your right arm and grab the halter. This should feel like you are giving your horse a nice hug.

Keep your right arm over the horse's neck. Open the halter with both hands so that the horse's nose can easily enter the halter. Gently slide the halter over the horse's face.

the circle and chase it around until it redirects its attention to you. As soon as the horse's attention is back on you, repeat what you did previously. It is unlikely that the horse will come all the way to you at first, and you will eventually reach a point where you can no longer back away from the horse without running into a fence or other obstacle. As soon as you reach the obstacle, stop and stand for a moment. Give the horse time to stand and look at you. After a little time has passed, walk forward to the horse—not with the intention of catching it—and touch it on the shoulder. There is a chance your horse will leave at this point. If the horse does leave, repeat the entire process until you can walk up to the horse

with the halter in front of you and the horse does not leave.

Once you can actually walk up to your horse and pet it, it is important not to halter the horse. A lot of horses are hard to catch because they realize that when someone comes up to them with a halter, they are going to have a negative experience. Do not catch your horse and start working it right away. Go out with your halter and lead rope to pet the horse and then leave it alone. A lot of catch and release is good for horses. This process will allow your horse to see you as someone who is not just going to get it out, work it hard, and put it away. The horse will see you as someone who enjoys spending time with it.

Once you have the halter pulled onto the horse's face, you can tie it. Putting a halter on this way will make your horse easier to bridle, because the two activities are so similar.

continued from page 41

Once you can walk up to your horse with the halter in plain view and your horse stays where it is standing, you are ready to put the halter onto the horse. There is a large dispute within the horse world as to what kind of halter to put on a horse. Some people believe that the only kind of halter to use is a rope halter. Others believe that the only kind of halter to use is a nylon web halter.

Each halter has its benefits for different uses. On our ranch, we train horses only in rope halters, because these halters make horses more responsive with less effort on our part. If you were going to go bungee jumping, which harness would you pick—a flat, fat, nylon strap or a skinny, knotted rope? If you care at all for the well-being of your hind end, you would definitely pick the fat, flat, nylon strap. But when we are training, we don't want a horse to have a nice padded surface touching its face. The horse needs to be able to feel even the slightest pressure when the rope is pulled.

The beauty of a rope halter is that it is not strong enough to hurt the horse or be abusive. It is just right in terms of the amount of pressure you exert and the amount of pressure the horse feels. If it takes 20 pounds of pressure to back a horse in a rope halter; it takes about 60 pounds of pressure to back the same horse in a flat, nylon halter. Unless you are extremely strong, it is a good idea to train your horse in a rope halter.

We run into a lot of people who use a flat halter in the trailer, making it a little softer on the horse's face in case of a bump or jar. There is no problem with this type of use for a flat halter.

It is best to try both kinds of halters and see what works best for you. Use your own good judgment. However, we do not encourage the use of stud chains on horses in any circumstance. Stud chains are paired with a flat, nylon halter. They snap in on the right side of the horse's face, go under the chin, and go back out of the D-ring on the left side of the face. This setup creates a small loop around the horse's nose that will tighten when you pull on the chain. This small loop is highly aggressive and borders on abuse. If you want to get more feel from your horse or for the feel to be a little softer, use a rope halter instead of a mechanical solution.

Rope halters were originally inspired by a lariat around a horse's neck. The rope halter is most effective when it fits behind the horse's jaw. When you pull the horse forward, you are putting pressure on its jaw and poll instead of just the poll. This helps in making your horse respond faster when applying pressure.

Once your horse is safely haltered, it is time to make sure it leads respectfully. Horses show how they feel about the humans in their lives by where they put the humans in comparison to their own bodies. If you had a photographer take an aerial shot of you and your horse as you were leading it down a straight road, who would be leading whom? If you showed this photo to a non–horse person, would he or she say, "Oh, yeah, that horse is leading that human," or "That human is leading that horse"? If it looks like the horse is leading the human to you, then it will definitely feel that way to the horse. This situation is not healthy, because you want the horse to see you as its leader and to follow you.

There is a famous trainer in Spain who bases all his training on how the horse leads. He gets amazing results with hard, mean horses that have shown disastrous results with

Flat nylon halters, as seen on the chestnut horse, are comfortable for a horse. Whether you use a rope or a nylon webbed halter, make sure you do not tie your horse on the wrong side of the fence, as shown in this photo. If the gray horse were to pull back, he could quite easily rip both of the rails down. Always tie on the other side of the fence.

The opposite of having your horse pushing and running you over is what this horse is doing—balking. The horse will lead forward a few steps, stop hard, pull back on the lead rope, and refuse to move forward.

You fix this problem by continuing to hold your pressure and stepping off to the side of the horse. Horses are incredibly strong straight on but not nearly as strong off to the side. As soon as you get off to the side, continue your pressure.

As soon as the horse takes a step forward, release the pressure. Notice that when you release at just the right time, the horse does not just walk forward but trots forward.

51

If you are consistent and do not release your pressure when the horse stops and pulls back, you will have a horse that leads quite softly. We don't want horses to run up and crowd us. We also don't want horses to drag along behind us. Aim for something in between.

other trainers. He leads the horse in such a way that it is quite obvious to the horse that it is being led by the human. The trainer takes the horse from its owner and starts leading it up a hill. The whole way, he is constantly teaching the horse and reinforcing the message that the horse needs to get behind him and allow him to lead it. He will lead the horse for miles and miles, until he finally feels that the horse realizes that the human is the leader and the human is in charge. Once this happens, the trainer stops leading the horse, hops up onto it, and starts riding. Because he has taught the horse that he is the leader and

that everything is okay when the horse is with him, the trainer then has no trouble with the horse. He makes dramatic transformations in a lot of horse and human lives in a short amount of time—all by simply leading like a leader. When he returns riding a horse, the owner is usually completely shocked by the incredible transformation.

Ninety percent of horses do not lead appropriately in that they lead with the human trailing along at their shoulders. These horses are pushy and nervous because they feel there is no leader present and they need to fend for themselves. It is a powerful thing to

This horse is standing tied the way we want to see horses standing tied. It is being patient and is relaxed. It took a lot of time and practice to get this horse to look that nice when tied up. This horse is now to the point where you could leave it tied for hours. In those hours, the horse would sleep and never paw at the ground or get antsy. The horse has embraced tying as a job, and it knows how to do it well.

What if . . . my horse will not lead correctly?

If you are leading your horse along and it is constantly crowding your space, a good thing to do is to stop walking and let the horse run into you. Without turning around, back into your horse while rhythmically flapping your arms and stomping your feet. Continue backing into the horse until it backs up and out of your space.

Remember not to turn around and chase the horse, which will get undesirable results.

If a horse were to back into you, you would get out of its way, because you have respect for its hind end. But if it walked into you going forward, you would know that it wanted to be your friend. We want horses to see us in the same way and have respect for our backsides.

Once your horse is out of your space, lead it forward again. Walk a short distance. If you have done this exercise appropriately, the horse should stay back. As soon as you feel the horse begin to crowd you, stop walking and repeat the exercise. This is an easy way to keep your horse back out of your space and keep you in control of the space in front of the horse.

When you are training your horse, it is a good idea to allow it to see the world where it lives. The easiest and safest way to do this is to lead the horse. Take your horse for walks every day, but remember to keep the horse out of your space and make sure it knows who is leading whom.

This horse is leading nicely. However, the trainer begins to feel that the horse is slightly crowding him.

As soon as the trainer feels the horse crowding him, he stops his feet and allows the horse to bump into him. It is important that you stop your feet completely, so the horse understands that it did something wrong. If you started shaking your rope and got the horse to go back as you were walking, the horse would not know what it did wrong. When you stop, the horse realizes, "Oops! I just ran into him!"

Once the horse bumps into the trainer, he begins stomping his feet and rhythmically flapping his arms until the horse gets out of his space. We want our horses to see us as having a personal bubble that it is not okay to enter.

The horse is now leading quite respectfully and is no longer crowding the trainer. We can clearly see that the trainer is leading the horse, and the horse is not challenging him for leadership of the herd anymore. It is important to note that this in no way offends the horse. The horse looks as quiet as, if not quieter than before the trainer chased it out of his space.

This is what a lot of horses look like when they are initially tied to a trailer. This little mare wants to eat the grass and is not as patient as we would like, although she is still yielding to the rope. It is okay for horses to be emotional, as long as they do not lose control of their feet or have some form of tantrum.

teach a horse that you are in charge and to get back. Once the horse realizes that it is in the presence of a good leader, its entire emotional outlook will change. Horses are a lot like humans in this regard. When we feel we do not have a good leader, we worry, get uptight, and try to fend for ourselves. When we feel we have a good leader, we are relaxed and not worried about other things, because we trust that our leader will take care of us. As soon as your horse realizes it is in the presence of its leader, it will have a whole new outlook on the world. Things that were once scary will no

longer be scary, because the horse knows its leader will take care of it.

Believe it or not, tying is a fairly dangerous activity with your horse. A lot of people accidentally overwhelm their horses by tying them up to a fence too soon. The problem with tying is that it makes an absolute. Even if you tie your horse with a slipknot, it is hard to release the pressure and go with the horse if it becomes emotionally overwhelmed. You are taking away a prey animal's most primal response to fear: flight. It takes a lot of emotional and mental

Once the horse and trainer are in a safe place, the trainer stops the horse and stands back a few feet, so he is not supporting the horse. As you can see, the horse is free to go just about anywhere. If the horse stays still, it will do so because it wants to stay still, not because it is being forced. This is how it will behave when we finally leave it tied up and alone.

This colt quickly lost its patience with training and turned around to leave.

What if . . . my horse does not tie well?

If your horse does not tie well, start by taking it out with just a halter and lead rope. Leave the pen and find a place where your horse does not typically like to stand.

It is important that you do not do this exercise when your horse is relaxed; you need it to be agitated so that you can teach it something. If the horse is comfortable, it will stand around, and you won't be able to teach it how to be tied.

It is important that the spot you choose also be safe. You do not want any obstacles, such as a barbwire fence, broken-down machinery, or cars, since this exercise can be a bit emotionally taxing for horses.

Once you are in a safe place, stop your horse and step approximately 5 feet in front of it. Now comes the fun part. Make the horse stay standing right where you stopped it and do not let the horse eat. You will quickly get a picture of your horse's patience level. Most horses will stand for a minute or less and then try to eat. Do not let the horse eat, because when it is tied to a post or trailer, it will not be allowed to eat. If your horse steps forward, back it up. If your horse steps sideways, put it back where it came from.

It is important not to support the horse. It will be your most natural instinct to want to be next to the horse, holding onto the halter,

trying to soothe it with nice, calming words. It is important that the horse learns something here and that you do not just give it the answer. You might have a hard time learning things in school, and you never truly understand them until you figure them out yourself. It wouldn't do any good to have someone give you the answers. The same is true for your horse.

Continue putting the horse right back where it started, but do not move your feet. This exercise transfers directly into ground tying.

As soon as the horse is standing still and not moving, allow the belly of the rope to rest on the ground. If the horse moves, put it right back where it came from. There is no set amount of time to spend on this. Simply do the exercise until your horse acts like it could stand in that one place for hours.

All this training ties directly to controlling the feet. Once the horse's feet are under control and the horse shows no signs of having any issues with standing in one place for as long as you want, you are safe to begin tying.

As we said before, the problem with tying a horse is that it has no give and is an absolute. Loop the rope over the rail three or four times, so that if the horse does become overwhelmed, it will not hurt itself. Safe tying and patience

maturity on the part of the horse to remain where you put it and not try to get away. A horse is not ready to be tied if it is not good at leading or responsive on the halter. Tying is successful only if the horse is responsive to a lot of different pressures and shows a lot of maturity.

When you tie your horse, it is important to tie it in a way that is safe. A horse's center of gravity is located around its armpits. You

don't want to tie a horse on the same level as the center of gravity. If I asked you to push a wall over, you probably would not put your hands near your knees to push it over. You would also not reach up as high as you could to push it over, because your hands would not line up well with your center of gravity. Both horses and humans are most efficient when their power lines up with their center of gravity. If you wanted your horse to pull over

will slowly build over time, so do not expect to do this work in one weekend. Each horse is different. Some horses may be able to be tied within a week, while others may take months. The important thing is to stick with it and not lose your patience.

When these riders took a break for lunch, they tied up their horses far enough away from each other that they would not get into any trouble. When you are tying horses, be sure to give them plenty of room so they cannot bite or kick at each other.

a fence with the most pulling power possible, you would tie it close to its center of gravity. If you wanted your horse to have very little chance of getting away from the spot where it was tied, you would tie it high. If your horse was to pull back or try to pull away from where it was tied, it would be less likely to get away, because its strength would not be great enough. Horses get into the habit of pulling back and ripping away from where they are tied after being tied up once solidly, fighting it, and getting away. When this happens, the horse learns that the best answer when it is overwhelmed and tied up is to rip away.

When tying, do not allow the lead rope to be too long or too short. When the lead rope is too long, the horse tends to walk around too much and get itself into trouble. I've seen all kinds of crazy things, such as a horse stepping on its lead rope when tied to a

After the colt's small attempt at leaving, the trainer put the horse back where it started.

The colt is trying really hard to come up with a good answer to the problem. It has tried going left, going right, and turning around. This time, the colt is trying to back up. The trainer stays right where he is and continues to bring the colt back to where it started from.

As soon as the colt is back in its original spot and stops its feet, the trainer gives it complete relief from any pressure. This is done by laying the belly of the rope on the ground. After the colt tried everything it could think of to get away from the trainer, and the trainer kept putting it back where it started from, the colt realized the answer to the problem was to stand in place.

trailer, panicking when it couldn't get its head back up, and pulling the trailer over on top of itself. It is also bad, but not as dangerous, if the horse's rope is tied too short. Mostly, this is uncomfortable for the horse. It won't like the feeling of its head being hung. The best thing is have the rope long enough for your horse to stand relaxed and not have the rope pulling on its head. Should the horse move away from the spot where it is tied, it will run into pressure. But as soon as the horse goes back to the original spot, the pressure will release. If the horse runs into pressure every time it moves, this will encourage it not to move around. The horse will seek the relief of the only place it can

> A horse's center of gravity is located around its armpits. You don't want to tie a horse on the same level as the center of gravity.

put its head without running into pressure. This is the key to making and keeping a horse good about being tied.

The appropriate way to tie your horse finishes with using the correct knot. You always want a quick-release knot for tying a horse. A quick-release knot can do just that—release quickly. As with anything around horses, safety is a major concern. You need to be able to free your horse on a moment's notice if it is becoming panicky. Begin by looping your rope twice around a post or rail on a fence. A post is preferable to a rail. Posts are dug into the ground and are secure, whereas a rail is nailed to a post. Rails are also thinner than posts and break more easily. If you do tie a

A lot of people tie their horses this way. The problem is that the horse can easily walk forward and step over the lead rope. This can make for quite a wreck, especially if the horse is tied solidly to something besides a fence.

The first step in tying a horse to a fence is to loop the rope at least twice around the correct side of the rail or post. This will help your knot stay tied and keep it from sucking down onto itself. If the knot sucks down onto itself, it will no longer be quick release.

horse to a rail, do not tie it on the side with nails, because if the horse were to pull back, it could easily pop the nails loose and pull the entire rail down. Tie your horse on the side opposite the nails, so that if the horse does panic and pull back, it will just pull the rail into the post and not pull it off the fence. The rail can still break, but this is not nearly as bad as having your horse running around with an entire rail tied to it. By tying to a post, you will help ensure that your horse will be there when you return.

If your horse has pulled back in the past, it will pull back again. This is the unfortunate thing about horses. Once they have an answer that works for the problem of feeling trapped, they will continue using it for the rest of their lives. I know top horsemen with horses that pull back from time to time but are

> **Learning how to keep your horse from pulling back usually entails learning what triggers this reaction, working around it, and being ready if the horse does get scared and pulls back.**

63

You are going to create a loop with the tail of your rope. The simplest way to create the loop is to twist your rope. Grab the tail of the rope, with your thumb toward the end of the rope, and rotate your hand until your palm is up. Make sure the loop has the tail of the rope to the outside of the knot.

Reach farther down on your rope and create a smaller loop.

The little loop will go around the section of rope that is tied to the horse's head and then pass through the big loop.

Pull on the little loop to tighten the knot. When you tie the knot, make sure you do not stick your fingers into places where they will get caught if the horse suddenly pulls back.

To make this into a knot that your horse cannot easily untie, simply create another loop with the tail of the rope, run it through the existing loop, and pull the tail of the rope through the final loop. This knot is easy for you to untie but will not allow the horse to easily free itself.

otherwise great horses. For some reason, it gets ingrained into their minds that pulling back is the answer to their problems. I have seen people try all kinds of methods to get a horse to no longer pull back, but all are dangerous and none work forever. The best thing to do if your horse does pull back is to wrap your lead rope around the rail and not tie it up solidly to anything. If the horse does pull back, it will meet with resistance but not anything solid. The horse will be able to get away without hurting itself. This is fine when you are at home, but be extra cautious in a different environment. Learning how to keep your horse from pulling back usually entails learning what triggers this reaction, working around it, and being ready if the horse does

get scared and pulls back. It is good to just accept some things as the little quirks that make your horse special.

Groundwork

Many people buy into the misconception that groundwork is something you go out and do. Groundwork should start the second you pull your horse out of the pen and should continue throughout your entire interaction with the horse. People make horses crazy by going at groundwork like some sort of chore or physical training exercise. Groundwork is just a normal part of daily life with your horse. Catching, leading, and putting your horse away when you are done with it should all be done in a way that is beneficial to both you

If your horse is prone to pulling back, loop your rope around the rail. Then if the horse does get overwhelmed and pull back, it will not hurt itself by being tied solidly to the fence. Looping the rope creates enough resistance that your horse will stay where you put it and will not be able to stick its head down and eat.

and your horse. From the time you see your horse in the morning to the time you put it away, you are creating groundwork.

There are a lot of different groundwork exercises—both traditional, old-school training and fancy new natural horsemanship. I have seen exercises that are good from both groups. The important thing is to look at each exercise and evaluate it for both you and your horse. Ask yourself: What good is going to come from this for my horse, and what good is going to come from this for me? Determine whether or not the exercise is good for your horse first and for you second. As trainers, we want to put our horse's emotional and mental well-being over our desires and dreams. Remember, it is the relationship with your horse that comes first. If you choose

what works best for you first, you run the risk of hurting your relationship with your horse. Always do exercises that emphasize response and not reaction on the horse's part and that help you with making your horse more responsive. As you are doing exercises with your horse, watch the attitude of the horse. Attitude is everything in training. Imagine a child who did what was requested but grumbled about how much he or she didn't like you during the entire activity. As a parent, you would not like this situation, and it would worry you. Similarly, if a horse is doing the desired action but is doing it with a poor attitude, the training is a complete waste of time. Watch the attitude of your horse as you are working it. Signs of poor attitude are pinning of the ears when you ask it to do

Even though we are only exiting the horse's pen, we are still training the horse. Every interaction with the horse is an opportunity for training.

something, wringing its tail, or flipping its head. These signs are extremely bad and mean that you need to look at the way you are doing your groundwork, so you can improve the relationship with your horse.

Each exercise has its own benefits, risks, and rewards, so weigh each one carefully before attempting anything. It is never a good idea to start something you cannot finish, especially when you are training a horse. In the same breath, do not be so prideful as to continue an activity that is detrimental to you or your horse. As long as you have carefully evaluated each exercise and it makes sense to do it, it is probably a good thing to do. Here are a few simple exercises to help build your relationship with your horse. They are by no means the only exercises out there, nor are they necessarily perfect for you and your horse. It is up to you to ensure that each one is something you want to attempt. The more you do these exercises, the easier it will be to get the horse to do what you want by simply using pressure on its lead. Remember to be patient. If you get frustrated, take a step back and go at it with a fresh viewpoint.

The following exercises are the core of all the groundwork we do. As you do the exercises, be sure to go through the three phases of pressure: asking, telling, and following through. These three phases are the key to training horses. The easiest way to build resentment in any animal or human that you are trying to teach or train is to not go through the three phases of pressure in the right order. First ask politely, "Will you do this for me?" Then say, "You are going to do this for me." Finally, follow through with what you have just told the animal or human to do. You can ask, tell, or follow through with your horse with the amount of pressure you are putting on its

lead. People get into trouble when they feel bad about following through on what they have just said. So they ask, then tell, ask again, and then tell, hoping for a change but not getting one because they do not back up what they are saying. Make sure that your yes means yes and your no means no. By this we mean that if you ask your horse to do something, stick with it until it does the desired action. The three phases of pressure change as far as the amount of time and severity of the pressure, depending on the situation and the horse. Sometimes ask, tell, and follow through will be a quick progression, lasting only about a second in ask and tell, then staying strong on follow through until the horse does the desired action. Other times, ask will be slow and deliberate. The same goes with tell. The important part is that as soon as you get to follow through, you stick with it. As you are training and growing as a trainer, you will quickly realize how long each phase should last in each exercise. We cannot give you a defined scale for your pressure and time. It is just something you have to develop as you learn and grow.

Desensitizing

Desensitizing your horse will make the horse extremely safe and easy to be around. No one likes to be around a horse that is being flighty and snorty about every little thing that it sees. The problem is that it is only natural for a horse to be flighty and snorty about every little thing that it sees. As you are training your horse, look for things with which to desensitize your horse. Each time you find something that the horse is scared of, take the time to get the horse to where it is no longer fearful of that object. Each time you do this, you build trust and a stronger relationship with your horse. Desensitizing the horse is something that you will do for the entire relationship with the

Before you ask your horse to leave, it is important to start off in a neutral position. Notice that the belly of the rope is on the ground, creating no pressure for the horse.

When you are ready for your horse to move, begin with asking pressure. You can tell which way this cowboy is asking the horse to go. Notice that the belly of the rope is up off the ground and the cowboy is literally leading the horse's head off to the side.

horse, because horses are naturally prone to be flighty and be skeptical.

When you first introduce your horse to something it is scared of, it is important to do it in a way that is extremely safe for both of you. Begin by taking your horse into a safe working arena or round pen. Have the horse haltered with a 12- to 13-foot lead rope. Stand by your horse's left shoulder, with the lead rope running from the horse's head to your left hand, with all the rope coils in your right hand. Swing the rope with your right hand up and over the horse's back. Be careful to keep the horse's nose slightly tipped toward you so that if it were to react, it would pivot around its front feet and you could avoid getting run over. If the horse's nose is tipped away from you and you swing

the rope over its back, it is likely the horse will be scared and pivot on its front feet, but it will pivot its body toward you and run you over. As soon as you have swung the rope up and over the horse's back, begin pulling it off no matter what the horse is doing. As soon as you have the rope fully pulled off your horse, swing it up and over the horse's back again. Continue doing this until the horse stops its feet. As soon as the horse stops its feet, quit swinging the rope over its back and lead the horse forward a few feet. When you do this, you are telling the horse that it did the right thing. Allow the horse to pause for a moment, then begin again, but from the opposite side. You want to do this until you can walk in and swing your rope up over the horse's back without the horse reacting.

By showing the horse what is coming, you are telling the horse that it better start moving.

Follow through on what you ask the horse to do by twirling your rope at it. Within follow through, there are three phases of pressure. You start by twirling your rope at the horse. You move to lightly tapping the horse. From there you reach the most pressure, actually hitting the horse with the end of the rope.

Here the trainer is desensitizing the horse to a rope coming over its back. This exercise will help the horse accept other things, such as a saddle pad, saddle, and rider. We start off with the rope because it is light and easy to control. As you can see, the colt is agitated by this but is simply doing a turn on the forehand. This is the appropriate response to being agitated on the horse's part.

As soon as the horse stops its feet, the trainer immediately pets the horse and removes the rope from its back. This helps the horse learn that the appropriate response to fear is to stop its feet.

Use your creativity to come up with interesting ways to desensitize your horse. The more creative you are about getting your horse quiet about things, the safer the horse will be in the long run. When you introduce something new to the horse, make sure you introduce it in a safe way and that you follow the format of allowing the horse to move its feet in the appropriate way when it is upset. As soon as the feet stop, reward the horse by taking away the pressure. Using the format we have given you, you can easily desensitize your horse to anything from guns and tarps to plastic bags and hoses.

Lateral Longeing

Longeing seems to be a national pastime for horse people. The problem is that they are typically not doing it correctly. The two most important things in the way a horse longes are how the horse starts and how it stops. Everything else is just circles. People get hung up on how the horse looks in the circle, but that is of no importance compared to how well it starts and stops. If you train the horse to appropriately start and stop, it will perform its circles the way that you want it to, with its body curving to the inside.

When your horse starts, remember the three phases of pressure: ask, tell, and follow through. While facing the horse, ask the horse to go on the circle. Ask the horse to begin by pointing in the direction you wish it to go. Watch the horse's feet. If it walks forward and toward you, it has been doing its starts incorrectly. The appropriate response is

> The two most important things in the way a horse longes are how the horse starts and how it stops.

this with asking pressure, so just point your hand in the direction you want it to go. As you are training your horse, it will take more than just asking pressure at first, so you will have to build up through telling and possibly follow through. The way you tell a horse to go on the circle is by showing it the tail of your rope with your free hand. The follow through step is accomplished by twirling the rope toward the horse and eventually hitting it with the tail of the rope. No matter what

for the horse to step its front feet sideways, so its body is pointing the direction your hand is pointing. A horse should be able to do

Here we are being creative in desensitizing a horse. This horse is a little afraid of the red-and-white candy cane. The trainer continues to present the candy cane to the horse until it stops its feet. As soon as the horse stops its feet, the trainer removes the candy cane. The more you can show the horse that the things that scare it are really okay, the better off you will be.

73

A horse that is correctly lateral longeing will stay light on the rope even when it is out in the open. Notice that as the horse is going around the trainer, the trainer stands in the middle, not supporting the horse. When most people longe a horse, they constantly nag it to move forward. Once you get a horse going, allow it to do its job and correct it only if it changes direction or speed.

phase of pressure you are at, remember to stop when the horse moves its feet off to the side. If your horse walks forward into your space, which most horses probably will, shake your rope rhythmically and get the horse to back up. As soon as the horse backs up, start again with your pressure.

You can tell that a horse does not know what you are talking about by imagining yourself as the horse and me as the trainer. If I pointed for you to go to the left and you walked toward me, it would tell me that you did not understand what I was trying to say. The appropriate response from you would be to look in the direction I am pointing and then, if I continued pointing in that direction, to move your entire body in that direction. If you have performed this exercise correctly,

your horse will have performed a simple turn on the haunches. Once the horse is parallel to you and facing the direction you are pointing, take your hand down, and the horse should stay there. If you were to keep pointing, the horse should move in that direction.

After the horse has turned its front end and is parallel to you and facing the direction it is going to be moving in the circle, you can chase it forward. Most people don't realize that the drive line for a horse to move forward is from the point of the shoulder to about 1 foot in front of the nose. Many people believe that the drive line on a horse is from the point of the hip to 1 foot behind the butt. This zone is actually the stopping zone. If you were to apply pressure to this zone, the appropriate response from your horse would

When you ask your horse to start on the circle for lateral longeing, it is important that the horse responds by stepping its front feet over and away from you. It is really nice if the horse crosses its front feet as it steps over.

As soon as the horse is parallel to you, remove the pressure. If you point again, the horse should move forward.

be to yield its hind end and face you. You need to chase the front end of the horse to get your horse to move forward.

Horses, as they are going around you in a circle, should remain under complete control. I never let a horse run out of control around me. This increases the horse's anxiety and is in no way beneficial to the horse. I always make sure that I am in complete control of the horse's speed. Make sure the horse goes into the gait you want. Be a stickler for the appropriate speed and do not allow the horse to slow down or speed up out of that gait. Regulate the horse's speed by shaking your rope if it gets going too fast. If the horse is going too slow, chase it forward by twirling the end of your rope at its shoulder.

Equally important to the way a horse leaves you is the way it stops. There are many variations on how to stop a horse when it is going around you in a circle, and very few are correct. Here are two different ways to appropriately stop a horse when it is traveling around you in a circle.

The first method of stopping your horse is the one we typically use, because it keeps you in control and involves a turn on the forehand. Start by facing your horse as it travels around you. Once you are ready to stop the horse, tip your head toward the horse's rear end and start twirling your rope toward its butt. This may seem counterintuitive, because a lot of people are taught that to move a horse forward, you chase its hind end. But to the horse, you are asking it to disengage its hind end and turn to face you. As you are twirling the rope, slowly reel in the part of the rope that is connected to the horse's

When you are ready to stop the horse, begin by tipping your head toward its butt. The horse will feel that it is being pressured on its hind end.

Continue to tip your head and apply pressure on the hind end of the horse while slowly reeling it in. You are creating a smaller and smaller circle by reeling the horse in.

Eventually the circle will get so small that the horse will plant its front feet and stop by doing a turn on the forehand. The ultimate goal is to tip your hat toward the horse's rear and have it immediately yield its hind quarters.

head. This will make the circle smaller and smaller, encouraging the horse to stop. If you were to leave the rope long, the horse would circle around you faster and faster until it realized what you wanted. By making the circle smaller, you help the horse realize that you are asking it to yield its hind end. With the appropriate and perfect stop, you face your horse as it goes around and tip your head toward its rear end. The horse turns to face you and stops its feet. As the horse stops, it moves its hind legs around its front, completing a small turn on the forehand.

The second way to stop your horse is just like catching your horse when it is hard to catch. Start by facing your horse as it travels around the circle. Instead of chasing its hind end, stick your arm out as if to catch the horse. Step into the path of the horse. It is important to step a few feet in front of the horse—at least half the circle—so that the horse has ample opportunity to respond. As soon as you see your horse start to look at you, drop your arm to your side and quickly walk backward, being careful not to trip or fall into the fence. When you walk backward, you are naturally encouraging the horse to come to you. This is similar to catching the horse when it does not want to be caught, but this time we have a rope on the horse. If your horse is hard to catch, this is a great game to play, because you have your rope to help you. With a horse that is really timid and does not come up to you with confidence, spend a lot of time backing away from it and having it follow. If your horse is really pushy, do not spend a lot of time backing away from it. Instead, step into the horse and get it to

> If your horse is really pushy, do not spend a lot of time backing away from it. Instead, step into the horse and get it to get leave your space. This will help your horse lose its pushiness.

get leave your space. This will help your horse lose its pushiness. This method of stopping the horse should be done after your horse correctly and consistently stops using the first method.

Each time you stop your horse, it is important to pause and allow the horse to have a break. Do not continually stop and quickly change directions. You can do this once you have developed the horse, but at first, make sure to give your horse a lot of time to savor the feeling of being stopped. The thing that makes music sound beautiful is the pause between the notes. If someone were to play a song with no pauses in the music but constant note after note, you would find it rather irritating, and the music would have no true movement. The same thing goes for training a horse. It is the pauses in between the exercises that make the horse into a great horse. This time also gives your horse the opportunity to think and allows your training to sink in.

After you and your horse have had a nice, reflective moment, it is safe to go ahead and send the horse in the other direction. Be a real stickler for appropriate starts and stops. Don't spend too much time worrying about the way the horse goes around you. As you develop the way your horse starts and stops, the way it goes around you will improve as well. It is important to not turn this exercise into a way of wearing down your horse. You want to keep it fun. It should not be a chore for the horse. If at any time it seems like your horse is getting bored with going around in circles, add obstacles to make it more entertaining for you and your horse. Add a

When the trainer is ready to stop the horse, he will reach out with his arm as if to catch the horse. Then he will step in front of the horse to head it off.

As soon as the horse turns and faces the trainer, he lowers his arm and begins to back up.

Notice the way the horse is coming in to the trainer. The horse looks very interested in the trainer and what he is doing.

As soon as the horse reaches the trainer, he stops to pet the horse. This gives the horse a moment to savor being in the center of the circle. When this method of stopping the horse on a circle is done perfectly, there should be no pressure on the rope at any point.

It is easy for horses to become bored while lateral longeing. It is always nice to add some obstacles to prevent boredom. This horse seems to enjoy jumping over a log.

After a little while, the horse became bored with the log. The trainer took the horse to this embankment and allowed it to run up, along the fence, and then back down. These sorts of things will keep your horse entertained. They will also help the horse build up its athleticism.

log for the horse to jump over, cones for the horse to go around, or barrels for the horse to go over. Another way to make circles more interesting is to take the horse into the open. Find an odd spot that the horse is not used to and do your lateral longeing there. The more creative you get, the more you will be able to build the relationship with your horse by overcoming obstacles together.

If you are correctly doing the starts and stops, you will quickly realize that you have just taught your horse to turn both on the

forehand and on the haunches. When the horse leaves you, it should be doing a turn on the haunches. When the horse stops and turns toward you, it should be doing a turn on the forehand.

An easy way to mess up this exercise is to make your horse reactive instead of responsive. Make sure that your hands are not too heavy and that you are not scaring the horse or making it react to what you are doing. It is easy to force a horse into doing this exercise by hitting it with too much force too quickly. When you do this, your horse does not respond to you, it reacts. You want to watch the attitude behind the action and not just the action itself. Make sure your horse is responding to the pressure and not reacting to your cues.

Sidepassing

If your horse is good at starting going into a circle and stopping by yielding its hind end, then when you add the two together (chasing the forehand and then the haunches), your horse will sidepass.

Start by taking your horse into a pen with a tall, long fence. If the fence is too short, you will constantly be running into corners. If the fence is too low, your horse may be tempted to jump over it. Walk up to the fence until you are an arm's length away from it. Lead your horse with you on a 12- to 13-foot lead rope. Turn around and face your horse. Your horse should be parallel to the fence. Start your horse as if you are starting it on a circle that would run into the fence. The horse will do a half circle before it reaches the fence. Once the horse reaches the fence, it will probably stop. The typical reaction for the horse is to turn and face you. If your horse does this, it is not a problem. Point and act like you are chasing the horse off in a circle toward the fence. Your horse will probably give you a look that says, "Why do you want me to jump the fence?" Put your pressure on the shoulder of the horse and get it to step away from you, so it ends up perpendicular to the fence. It is very important that you reward even the slightest sideways motion, so that you don't teach your horse to flip over or jump the fence. Apply pressure to the front until the front end moves over. As soon as

The first step in getting your horse to sidepass is sending it around you until it runs into the fence.

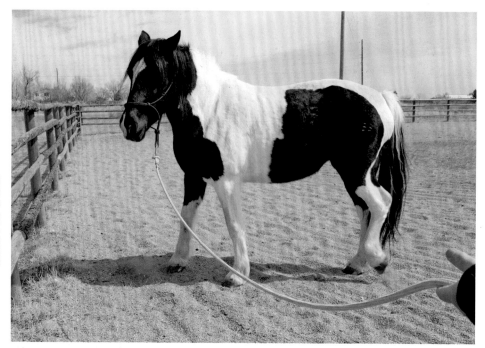

Allow the horse to walk into the fence, where it will most likely do a turn on the forehand and face you. This horse is moving its hind end away from the trainer as it runs into the fence.

Once the horse has stopped at the fence, the trainer can begin applying pressure to get the horse to sidepass. The problem is that the horse moved its hind end away from the trainer when it stopped, so it is not perpendicular to the fence. The trainer must apply pressure to the front end to get the horse perpendicular to the fence.

Once the front end of the horse has moved over, the hind end is too close. The trainer applies pressure to just the hind end to get it away from him.

Now that the horse has sidepassed well along the fence, it is time to take it out into the open. You will quickly realize that moving sideways is a combination of a turn on the forehand and a turn on the haunches. In this photo, the horse's hind end is lagging behind its front. The trainer is tipping his hat toward the horse's rear and chasing it to get over.

your horse makes one step in the appropriate direction, stop, pet the horse, back up, and start the same exercise in the opposite direction.

There is no designated single spot to apply pressure for the sidepass. The most important thing is to put pressure on the part of the horse that is pointed most at you. It will either be the front or the hind end. A horse will typically lead with one-half of its body in the sidepass, meaning that its hind end or front end will be pushed farther away from you. Add pressure to whichever part is closer to you, switching between the front and hind end as needed. If you apply pressure to the front and the horse turns away from you with its butt in your face and its nose going down the rail, you will know that your rope is too long. Your rope is your safety net. Make sure it is not too long, because it will allow the horse to get a good kick angle. Don't be surprised if this exercise is a bit agitating for your horse. Be ready for the horse to do something unexpected, since you are asking a lot from the horse and for a lot of yielding, which can be rather agitating as the horse is learning. It is important not to push the horse too far in this exercise. If you push your horse too far, it will do something dangerous. At first, stick to asking for a few steps in each direction and slowly build from there. This is a great exercise for increasing softness and control in your horse. The more you can control all four feet, the better off you will be. Sideways is not a motion that a lot of horses are good at or typically enjoy doing. Take it slow and easy and make sure to keep the exercise fun. Your horse will eventually be sidepassing like a dream.

Once your horse is good at sidepassing at the fence, try sidepassing in the open. Remember that your horse will try to walk forward. All you have to do is shake your rope. Stop and back the feet up each time they move forward. This will discourage forward motion. When you are sidepassing your horse in an open space, imagine that you are sidepassing it along an invisible fence. Make sure not to let the horse walk forward through your invisible fence.

Backing

All horses need to be able to go left, right, forward, backward, and sideways. So far, we have shown you how to get your horse moving left, right, forward, and sideways. Now comes the most important one of all: backward. There is an old saying: "The better a horse goes backward, the better it will go forward." We want to emphasize this idea in training. Horses should spend a lot of time in reverse, especially horses that don't have the best brakes. Remember, the opposite of forward is backward, not stopping. People are constantly telling me that their horses cannot physically back up. They have tried everything, but the horses will not go backward. This is an excuse that horse people use to make themselves feel better. The truth of the matter is that every horse can walk backward, and even trot and canter backward. The true question is whether or not you have the capability to train the horse to go backward. Instead of saying that a horse cannot go backward, people should say they cannot teach the horse to go backward. You cannot be saved until you truly know you are lost. When lifeguards learn how to save people who are drowning, they learn that you cannot save someone who is trying to save him- or herself. You have to wait until he or she is ready to be saved. Your training with your horse is not just about the emotional development of the horse. It is also about your own development as a person and a trainer.

There are three different things to watch for as you are backing your horse. The first is the horse's foot motion. How steadily does the horse move its feet backward? The second is the horse's head height. Does the horse go backward with its head up and nose out? The third is the most important: softness. Can you back up your horse with the slightest asking pressure on the halter? A good way to tell if a horse trainer knows what he or she is doing is to watch the person back up the horse. First, when the person asks the horse to back up using the reins, does the horse move its feet backward? Second, when the horse does move backward, what happens to its head carriage? Third, does it look like the person is pulling with all his or her might to get the horse to move its feet? When people pick up the reins to back up a horse, the head typically goes up and the nose goes out. This is the complete opposite of what we want horses to do. We want the head to come down when we pick up the reins, and the nose to tuck in. As you

This is the appropriate place to grab your horse's halter when you are teaching it to back up. Neutral is with your hand pointed straight down. Ask is with your hand pointed toward the rear, with slight pressure. Tell is more pressure, and follow through is all your pressure.

When you are backing your horse, make sure you move your feet with the horse, so you can stay in position. Horses tend to get frustrated when you begin to back them, so keep your arm ready as a block in case the horse tosses its head.

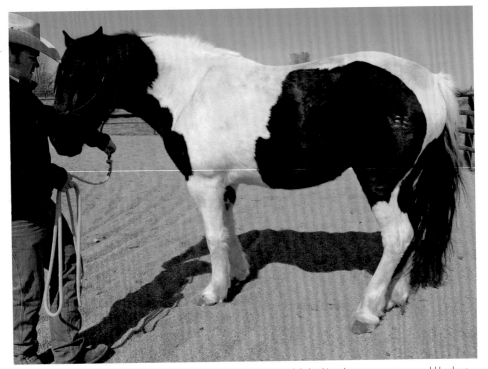

Here we have backed our horse into a corner. You get the horse to turn while backing the same way you would back up a truck.

By bringing the horse's head to the left, the trainer is able to get the horse's hind feet to go to the right.

It is good to not simply back your horse in a straight line but also to do a few turns while backing. This helps increase your control and teaches your horse to yield to some different pressures.

are backing your horse from the ground, keep a close watch on these things and try to encourage them as you are working.

The first step in backing up your horse is to go to the horse's left side and grab the bottom of the halter where the rope snaps into it. Make sure to grab there and not on the rope. If your hand is on the rope, it will bump into your horse's chest and make it difficult to have any leverage as you go through the three phases of pressure. When you grab the halter, make sure your thumb is pointing toward the ground. Slowly apply downward and backward pressure. Make sure you gently go through the three phases of pressure. It may seem like we are constantly talking about this "ask, tell, follow through" thing. That's because it is the core of your training and everything you do with your horse. If you don't learn anything from us other than ask, tell, and follow through, we (and your horse) will be happy.

As soon as your horse moves a hoof backward, release your pressure. It is very important to release pressure only when the horse moves backward, not forward or to the side. A lot of people have a hard time with this next part, especially as they get frustrated. Make sure to stay relaxed and remember that you are teaching. Start over with your pressure, beginning with ask. People often forget this and go right back to the pressure they were applying when the horse finally moved its foot. If you do this, you will frustrate your horse. Imagine that someone asked you to clean your room, but you didn't clean it. Then the person told you to clean your room, and you did. The next time your room needed cleaning, the person told you to clean it rather than asking, because telling was the amount of pressure needed to get you to clean your room the first time. This is a natural-born recipe for resentment. You deserve the opportunity to respond to asking

pressure. The same thing goes for your horse. Do not assume that since it took tell pressure last time, it will take tell pressure this time. Always give your horse the opportunity to move off the lightest asking pressure.

Another mistake you can make with your pressure is being wishy-washy. An example is starting with ask pressure, going to tell, going back to ask, and then going to follow-through pressure. The horse still doesn't move, so you go back to ask pressure. This sort of training never works. Consistency, along with proper escalation through the phases of pressure, is the key.

Once you have your horse moving its feet backward smoothly and in a consistent manner, you need to start worrying about head carriage. Apply steady pressure and do not release until the horse's head comes down. As soon as the horse's head comes down as it is moving backward, release the pressure. Once your horse moves its feet backward fluidly and brings its head down and in, it should be pretty soft on the halter, because the entire time you have been working on making sure the horse is soft. All three elements should come together to create a horse that is responsive and easy to back up.

One-rein Stops

When taught appropriately from the start, the one-rein stop is the ultimate in emergency brakes. We know people who have had the one-rein stop save their lives on more than one occasion. The one-rein stop is also extremely useful in increasing flexion in your horse, improving your stops, and teaching the horse to yield off your legs so that you can turn on the forehand from in the saddle.

We do this exercise by going to the horse's left side, standing at its front left leg, and facing its body. With your right hand, reach on top of the withers and grab a small handful of mane. You should also have the tail of your coiled rope in your right hand. With your left hand, grab the lead rope just below the snap.

It is very important to stay in this position as your horse goes around. The odds are that your horse will try to move in a circle, go forward, back up, or sidestep away from or toward you. Any of these reactions is normal, but it is important to stay with the horse and not let it get you away from the position you are in right now. You will need to move your feet to do this. With your hand on the withers, you will be able to tell the direction your horse is going to be moving—away from or toward you—so you should be ready to move with the horse. People become very goal oriented when they perform this exercise and do not

stick to the principle. It is important to be principle oriented while training your horse. The principle in this exercise is that as soon as your horse bends its neck, even a little bit, you release the pressure. Your ultimate goal is to be able to pick up the rein and have the horse reach all the way around with its nose until it touches its own shoulder or side. This is not something your horse will be doing on the first day, but it is the ultimate goal.

Start by applying pressure with your lead rope and pull your horse's head around toward you. Make sure to go through all three phases of pressure, starting with ask and proceeding to follow through. Most of the time, the horse will spin like a top and go

When you are teaching your horse to do a one-rein stop, make sure to get a good hold on the horse, with your anchor hand up on the withers. No matter what this horse does when the trainer pulls the one-rein stop, he can easily stay in this position.

When you first pull a one-rein stop, you will notice that the horse does not bend all that far around. That's okay. This is a good starting spot.

As the horse becomes more developed with its one-rein stops, it will be able to bend its neck all the way around and touch its belly with its nose.

As with all training, release pressure as soon as the horse gives the desired outcome. Notice in this photo that the trainer did not have enough slack in his rope to be able to fully release the horse's head. He could release it only partially. This is not a major mistake, but it is still a mistake. Make sure that when you release the horse's head, you are able to give it its head fully.

around in circles. Stay with the horse in that position and allow it go around you until its feet stop moving. If the feet stop and there is still pressure on your rope, do not release

> The one-rein stop is also extremely useful in increasing flexion in your horse, improving your stops, and teaching the horse to yield off your legs so that you can turn on the forehand from in the saddle.

the pressure until your horse bends its neck and releases the pressure on the rope. Do not release the pressure if the horse is still moving its feet or pulling on the rope. As soon as the horse is standing still and has released the pressure by bending its neck, immediately give the horse the rope back. Take a moment and tell the horse how smart it is and then start the exercise again.

Each time you perform this exercise, the goal is for the horse to bend its neck farther around, keep its feet planted, and stay light on the rein pressure. This is a good exercise to do from both sides of your horse.

SADDLING YOUR HORSE

We are now going to explore the proper way to put a saddle on your horse. This method is safe and easy for both you and the horse. The most important thing in saddling your horse is to make sure it is emotionally and mentally prepared. You want to use your understanding of the nature of horses to make saddling an easy event in a horse's life. If you do a good job of preparing the horse, you can avoid problems such as pulling back and flipping over.

Notice that this horse is in a safe area with no real obstacles. If the horse were to have a tantrum, it would be easy for the rider to control the situation and remain safe.

When approaching your horse with the saddle pad, keep the pad down low and still until you are in the proper position to introduce it to the horse. The proper position is standing approximately 1 foot in front of the shoulder, with a small amount of slack in the rope. If your horse is startled by the pad, it can move away from and around you instead of on top of you.

This horse is quite relaxed about the feel of the saddle pad on her back. Once your horse looks contented like this, you are ready to place a saddle on its back. Make sure your horse is good at this exercise from both the left and right sides.

What if . . . my horse will not stand still to saddle?

The first step in getting your horse to stand still to saddle is performing the same exercise used to desensitize the horse to objects. Take your horse into an open area where it is free to move its feet without any obstacles nearby. Have the horse haltered with a 12- to 13-foot lead rope.

Stand on the horse's left side at the shoulder, with your rope running from the horse's head to your left hand and with all the rope coils in your right hand. With your right hand, swing the rope up and over the horse's back. Be careful to keep the horse's nose slightly tipped toward you, so that if the horse were to react, it would pivot around its front feet and you could avoid getting run over.

Follow the horse and, unless it is headed for danger, continue swinging your rope onto its back and pulling it off again. As soon as the feet stop, quit swinging the rope onto its back and step back. At this point, be sure to tell your horse how smart it is.

If you have good timing when you stop, the horse will stand still when you walk in to swing the rope onto its back the second time. If the horse doesn't stand still, continue with the exercise until it does.

Continue doing this until both you and especially your horse are bored with the exercise. If your horse has a lot of difficulty with this exercise, revert to the section on sacking out and desensitizing your horse. If you correctly completed that portion of your groundwork, this task should come quite easily.

Use a rope to start desensitizing your horse to the feel of a saddle. Make sure to be nice and big with your movements. It is very important not to sneak through this phase of your horse's training and development.

This horse decided he didn't like the feel or look of me throwing the rope up over his back. He then decided he was going to get away from me. I kept gently throwing the rope over his back as he moved.

Once your horse stops his feet, take the rope off his back. This is a good point to tell your horse how smart he is and give him a nice rub on the neck. The most important part of training your horse is stopping. The horse learns a lot when you leave him alone or quit the stimulation.

When you are putting a saddle on your horse for the first time, you want to ensure that the horse can move its feet. Horses express themselves with foot motion, and if the horse is tied up, it will try to express itself, feel trapped, and become agitated. Horses are also prey animals and are therefore claustrophobic and prone to panic. The more you can remember these facts and accommodate your horse's natural way of being, the happier and safer your relationship with your horse will be.

Once you can swing your rope onto the horse's back from either side and it stands still to the point of borderline sleeping, it is time to introduce the saddle pad. Do the same exercise you did with the rope, but this time

with the saddle pad. When you first introduce the saddle pad, do not lay it completely across your horse's back. Start by laying it only on its left side, so that if the horse gets scared it will move away from you and not on top of you. Do this exercise until you can throw the saddle pad onto your horse from either side and not have it react. If you want your horse to be good at anything, such as saddling, tying, or catching, the best thing to do is to repeat the process often. Do not just saddle the horse when you want to go for a ride. Get your horse out, saddle it, unsaddle it, and put it away, so the horse does not always associate saddling with work.

An easy way to gauge a horse's mental well-being is to look at what its feet are

Approach your horse with the saddle and always keep an eye on the horse. As long as the horse continues to look relaxed, continue to walk closer with the saddle.

The proper way to place a saddle on your horse's back is to first get into the horse's safe zone. Pet the horse and let it know you are there. Once your horse looks relaxed, turn your back to the horse, with your rope in the crook of your left arm. Grasp your saddle by the pommel with your left hand and grasp the cantle with your right.

To get your heavy saddle up onto your tall horse, swing the saddle around and let centrifugal force help you get it onto the horse's back.

Using centrifugal force to lift a saddle above your head is much easier than cold lifting. Notice that the horse is looking at something, but its feet are not moving. We want horses to be free to look at things, as long as their feet stay under control.

This is a safe and quietly saddled horse.

What if . . . I can't throw my saddle onto my horse's back?

When you are first learning to throw your saddle onto your horse's back, you may accidentally whack the horse's side or legs with a flying stirrup or the whole saddle.

A good way to practice saddling that will not hurt your horse is to find a fence that is approximately the same height as your horse. Pretend the fence is your horse and practice swinging your saddle onto it.

doing. If the horse's feet are moving, you do not want to saddle your horse. The same rule applies if the horse is mentally locked up. People sometimes have a hard time telling the difference between a horse that is standing still and one that is mentally locked up. A mentally locked-up horse is easy to distinguish by the look on its face and the carriage of its body (refer to the discussions of horse behavior and reading your horse in the introduction). When a horse is locked up, it will do one of two things to come out of the state it is in. The horse will either go into a relaxed state or have some form of a tantrum. If your horse is mentally locked up or its feet are continually moving, it is not safe for the horse to be tied or for you to try to saddle it. See the "What if . . . my horse does not tie well?" sidebar in Chapter 1.

The appropriate saddle pad is important to the mental well-being of your horse. Imagine walking around in cowboy boots with no socks; it would not feel very good. The same is true for the saddle and saddle pad. We recommend that you purchase a saddle pad that is nonporous on the horse side, so that the saddle pad does not soak up the horse's sweat. Sweat is your horse's cooling mechanism. If the sweat is absorbed by the saddle pad, it does not cool the horse as intended. The pad can also cause sores if your horse is carrying pounds of sweat on its back. A nonporous pad will put the sweat where it belongs—on your horse's back and dripping down its front.

Another important aspect of saddling is saddle placement. Many people place their saddles too far forward. Think about your own body for a second. Reach around to your upper back and feel one of your scapulas. Push on the scapula and rub your hand back and forth. That is what it feels like for your horse to have a misplaced saddle. Feel your horse's back where you would normally place the saddle. Feel for the horse's scapulas just as your felt for your own. As your horse moves, these bones move, similar to you moving your arms. When you have the saddle and pad set on the horse's back, move them right behind the scapulas. It might take some getting used to, because this is farther back than people are normally accustomed to. You will notice a change in your horse. It will be happier and better behaved when it isn't in pain caused by improper saddle placement.

Be ready for an exciting experience the first time you cinch up your horse! When a horse first feels a cinch being tightened around its body, it has a tendency to panic. To set yourself up for success in cinching, be sure that your horse is settled and ready for you to put on the pad and saddle. You also must make sure the horse is not tied, because it needs to be able to express itself freely and safely.

Take your horse into a safe place and put your saddle pad and saddle onto its back in their appropriate positions. If you have done

Once the saddle is safely placed on your horse's back, make sure the saddle is in the proper position. Feel under the saddle for the rear edge of the scapulas. Place the leading edge of the saddle tree right behind the edge of the scapulas.

your homework correctly, the horse will be standing in a relaxed state of mind. This will be evident in its posture and still feet. Go to the other side of your horse and let down the cinch. Return to the left side. Have the rope in your left hand with slack. While not pulling on the halter, reach under your horse's belly and grab the cinch with your right hand.

The entire time you are cinching your horse, pay close attention to its mental and emotional state. If you notice a change in the horse, be sure to stay cautious and light on your feet until your horse relaxes. It is good to push the horse a little bit, but do not push it to the point where it explodes, especially when beginning saddling. Pull up the slack on your cinch until the horse can feel the pressure. Immediately release the pressure of the cinch once the horse has felt it. Now pull up on the cinch again. Continue doing this until you can put pressure on the cinch and the horse doesn't react at all. Once you can pick up the cinch and put it under the horse's belly and there is no reaction, loosely wrap your latigo twice. Pull up the cinch with the latigo so that the cinch is tight enough to hold the saddle in place should the horse move around. Lead

your horse off at a 45-degree angle so that it is able to move with the saddle.

Once your horse has taken its first few steps in a calm and safe manner, stop and tighten the cinch a little bit more. Repeat the leadoff from the 45-degree angle from the other side. Allow the horse to walk a few steps and tighten your cinch some more. Make sure you do not tighten the cinch all at once, especially with a young or inexperienced horse. If you cinch up your horse all at once, the horse will be overwhelmed. A side effect is that your horse will blow its stomach out to where it feels like the saddle is tight. Once you get on the horse and move around, the horse will let that air out, and your saddle will be loose. Some people believe the way to fix this blowing-out problem is to cinch up the horse tight all at once. After the cinch is tight, they punch the horse in the stomach, making it blow out all its air. Then they tighten up the cinch some more. Horses obviously do not appreciate this method of handling, and neither do we.

A bad way to check if the cinch is tight is to stick your fingers between the horse's skin and the cinch. This tells you nothing and

What if . . . my saddle does not fit correctly?

A practical way to see if your horse's saddle fits well is to do this simple check at the end of your ride. Once you are finished riding for the day, check your horse's sweat pattern underneath the saddle.

If your horse has a good, even sweat mark across its back, the saddle is a good fit. There will be more sweat in places where there is more pressure and less sweat in places where there is less pressure. If your horse's sweat mark has

wet spots in the front and back but a relatively dry spot in the middle, your saddle is bridging across its back and is therefore uncomfortable. If the sweat mark is uneven, you'll know that the fit is not good for your horse.

An easy way to fix a poor-fitting saddle is to add saddle shims to fill the empty space where the saddle is bridging. The shims are typically 1/4-inch-thick pieces of felt, available at most tack shops.

pushes the horse's hair up so that it is not lying flat against its body, which increases the potential for sores. The appropriate way to make sure the cinch is tight is to reach up, grab the saddle horn, and gently rock the saddle back and forth. If the saddle does not feel solidly connected to your horse, you need to continue tightening the cinch.

When you are training a horse, make sure the horse is used to the cinch around its stomach before you worry about the flank

Once you have your horse ready to take its first steps with the saddle on, make sure you are safe, in case the horse is overwhelmed and has a tantrum. Notice that this horse is walking forward but is not going to walk to the handler. When you are on a 45-degree angle like this, you will be safer if your horse acts out. The horse will typically try to come to you if it is feeling overwhelmed. Continue to stay on a 45-degree angle until the horse settles down.

cinch. Once the horse is quiet and easy to saddle, it is a good time to prepare your horse for a flank cinch. It is good for your horse to know the feel of a flank cinch, whether it is going to be used for English or Western riding. To get your horse used to the flank cinch, do the exact same procedure you did with the regular cinch. Remember that horses are generally ticklish around their flanks. Your horse should be at the point where it can walk around with a saddle and is not bothered by it.

Once you have placed your saddle onto the horse's back and have it securely cinched, it is important to go through all your groundwork while the horse is wearing the saddle. Saddling your young horse should be a daily occurrence. The horse should be saddled every time it is out of its paddock.

What if . . . my horse bucks when I saddle it?

Once your horse is saddled and the cinch is holding the saddle in place, step the horse off to the side at a 45-degree angle. This allows the horse, if it does choose to throw a tantrum, to throw the tantrum away from you and not on top of you. It is important that your saddle be cinched tight enough to stay place no matter what your horse does.

There are many different ways that the initial saddling can play out. Always plan for the worst and hope for the best. If your horse does choose to throw a fit, it will be within the first few steps. During a tantrum, keep yourself off to the side at a 45- to 90-degree angle, allowing the horse to move around with you as the center of the circle.

Your most important task when the horse is having a tantrum is to keep its nose tipped

toward you. If you keep the horse's nose tipped toward you, you will not lose the horse, and your chances of getting kicked are much less. Allow your horse to express itself freely, bucking and kicking all it wants.

Once your horse is finished feeling uncomfortable with the saddle, its feet will stop moving. Do not walk toward the horse or get in front of it. Always stay off to the side, so you will be safe if the horse decides to continue its expression of frustration. Once the horse stops moving its feet, let it stand still for a moment and start over. Continue this exercise until your horse will gently walk when you pull it forward while wearing the saddle. Once you get the horse to this point, it is important to give the horse a lot of time to feel the saddle on its back and the cinch around its midsection.

You do not want to actually put a bit into your horse's mouth the first time you bridle your horse. Even the best horsemen in the world can accidentally slip, or the horse can toss its head and ram the bit into its teeth, especially when you are first starting out. Whenever we teach a horse to bridle, we start by using a piece of 1/4-inch-thick rope tied into a loop the size of the bridle. Unlike a cold, hard bit, the rope is warm and soft, so that if the horse does throw its head, or if the trainer slips, the rope does not hurt the horse's teeth. Horses that throw their heads to bridle or unbridle have had their teeth hurt in the past by a bit coming in or out of their mouths. It is important to put a bridle on in the proper sequence so as not to hit the horse's teeth or crush its ears.

The appropriate way to bridle a horse is by going to the left side of the horse and placing your reins over the horse's head and around its neck. Once you have your reins around the horse's neck, you can take off the halter if you prefer, because you still have hold of the horse with the reins. Place your left hand, which is holding the top of the bridle, near the horse's forehead, with the bit under the horse's chin. Switch and put your right hand over the top of the horse's head and grab the bridle where your left hand was holding it, keeping the bit under the horse's chin. With your left hand, reach down, grab the bit, and gently set it at the horse's lips. Using your left thumb,

Start by taking the halter off the horse's nose and tying it around the horse's neck to keep control. Once you have the halter around the horse's neck, slip the reins up over its head.

Grasp the bridle by the top of the headstall with your left hand and bring it up above the horse's eyes toward the forelock.

open the horse's mouth and gently guide the bit into its mouth. Once the bit is in the horse's mouth and you are holding the bridle with your right hand, reach up with your left hand and grab the top of the bridle. Gently tip the right ear forward and into the headstall, and do the same with the left ear. The last step is to buckle up the throat latch. Bridling your horse in this way will help ensure your horse stays easy to bridle for the entirety of its life.

Once you have your horse bridled, it is important that you have the bit appropriately adjusted in the horse's mouth so that it is comfortable. If the bit is too low in the horse's mouth, it will knock into the horse's lower teeth. If the bit is too high in the horse's mouth, it will constantly be stretching the horse's face, be uncomfortable, and cause sores in the corners of the horse's mouth. Place the bit high enough to be out of the lower teeth but not so high as to stretch the corners of the mouth. There should be one or two wrinkles in the corner of the horse's mouth.

After your horse is easy to bridle with the rope and the actual bit, it is a good time to teach the horse to keep its mouth shut while wearing a bit. We do this with an old vaquero (cowboy) tradition that has been passed down through many generations. Snap your lead rope into the left side of the bit. Do all the groundwork that you have been practicing from the left side of the bit. Circle your horse to the left, then circle it to the right. Back the horse from the left side of the bit and get it to

Switch your hands so that your right hand is holding the top of the headstall and your left is tending to the bit under the horse's chin.

With your right hand holding the top of the headstall, use your left hand to guide the bit to the horse's mouth. Some horses will naturally open their mouths when they feel the bit, but some won't. If your horse won't open its mouth when you bring the bit up to its teeth, stick your thumb into the corner of its mouth. The horse will then open its mouth.

It is very important that you do not mash the horse's ears as you put them into the headstall. Gently tip the right ear forward and slip the headstall over it.

Once the headstall is over the right ear, gently tip the left ear forward and slip it into the headstall.

Remember to attach the throat latch. It keeps the bridle from falling off over the front of the horse's head.

bend its neck and yield to the pressure from the right and left side. You should be snapped into the left side of the bit during this entire process. You will notice that if you gently work with your horse with the bit in its mouth, using maneuvers it already knows, the horse will quickly learn to close its mouth on the bit. This method has good results and is sixteen times faster than just making the horse wear a bridle while it is tied. The horse will hold its mouth shut within the first minutes of the first session in most cases.

Bits

What activities you do with your horse will determine what type of bit you use. It is also important to consider where your horse is in its training when choosing your bit. Each horse is different, and age does not affect the bit you choose. Some owners may choose to ride without a bit and instead use a rope

What if . . . my horse throws its head when I am bridling it?

If your horse does not hold its head still to be bridled, stop bridling it with a bit and go back to bridling with the rope. It does not make a difference if your horse is older and has been riding for a long time. You still have to go back to the rope to fix this problem.

You need to identify what is making your horse throw its head. Is it because of the bit going into its mouth, or is it because of the way you are putting its ears into the headstall? If it is because of the bit going into its mouth, make sure the bit gently enters its mouth and does not hit its teeth. If you have been bonking the bit into its teeth for a long time, you will need to spend a lot of time bridling with the rope to reassure the horse that once you put something into its mouth, it will not hurt. If the problem is the horse's ears going into the headstall, make sure you are folding its ears while inserting them. Simply tip the entire ear forward from the base and slide it into the headstall.

Another bridling problem occurs when a horse raises its head so high that you can't reach it. The way to fix this problem is to teach the horse to lower its head. This is done by grabbing your lead rope just below the snap and pulling straight down toward the ground. Start slowly and add pressure as you go through the three phases of pressure. Once you reach the follow-through phase, hold steady with downward pressure. As soon as your horse gives its head even slightly to the downward pull, release and pet your horse, and repeat the process. Your horse will quickly lower its head to a working level if you are doing this process correctly.

If you bring the bridle in once the horse's head is down and it raises its head at the sight of the bridle, pull the horse's head back down. This is a good place for you to practice your patience and understanding. You may have to stick with this exercise for a long time before the horse finally keeps its head down.

If you have the bit in your horse's mouth, its head is down, you go to put an ear into the headstall, and the horse lifts its head, keep the bit in the horse's mouth by lifting up on the headstall. Grab the rope with your free hand and pull the horse's head back down to a working level. If your horse is bad about being bridled, it is important to leave your halter on for this process.

halter with a lead rope. It all depends on what use you have for your horse.

When training a horse, no matter its age, we always start off in a hackamore. The hackamore is a traditional Spanish tool that found its way up the California coast with the vaqueros. You can use a real hackamore or a halter with a lead rope. A hackamore is nice for young horses because it stays away from their teeth during the developing years, and it does not inhibit your riding. It is also good for older horses to help develop softness. The softer the hackamore, the more it encourages flexing. The stiffer the hackamore, the more it encourages straightness. We start horses in a soft hackamore or rope halter and move them into a stiffer hackamore as they progress.

Once your horse is riding nicely in a hackamore or rope halter, you can continue on to a snaffle bit. A snaffle bit is defined as any bit that does not have any leverage. We do not like to see people ride in what is

A very simple hackamore is a rope halter and a lead rope. This is a nice way of tying your rope to your halter so the tail does not whack your horse in the face. It also does not come untied until you want it to release.

called a shanked snaffle. People call certain bits shanked snaffles, but it is actually impossible for a snaffle bit to be shanked. If the bit has shanks, then it is a leverage bit and therefore not a snaffle. A shanked snaffle does what is called a nutcracker. Because of this nutcracker effect, you run the risk of crushing the bars of your horse's mouth when you ride in a shanked snaffle. The worst thing you can do when training is put a leverage bit into a young or inexperienced horse's mouth. The unshanked snaffle bit is good for bending and getting a horse used to the feel of a bit.

When you feel confident in your horse's comfort and your control with the snaffle, and your horse is not mouthing or chewing on the bit, you can continue to a bridle with a shanked bit. The shanked bit is a good tool for refinement, but it is neither safe nor good on a horse that is not ready for it. Every time I turn around, I see people riding in a shanked bit when they should be riding in a hackamore. The rider's hands are not developed, and the horse is not ready for the bit. Many people think a bigger bit results in bigger control. A bigger relationship with your horse is what actually results in bigger control. The shanked bit, when used appropriately, is the highest level of refinement and demonstration of relationship. A lot of people think that with a shanked bit, you neck rein your horse and turn the horse by laying your rein across its neck. This is incorrect. You use your legs to push your horse left or right and ride almost completely with your seat, barely ever touching your reins.

Parts of a Saddle

Tips for Saddling Your Horse

The most important thing in saddling your horse is to make sure it is emotionally and mentally prepared, as well as physically prepared. You want to use your understanding of the nature of horses to make saddling an easy event in a horse's life. When you are putting a saddle on your horse for the first time, you want to ensure that the horse can move its feet. Horses express themselves with foot motion, and if the horse is tied up, it will try to express itself, feel trapped, and become agitated. Horses are also prey animals and are therefore claustrophobic and prone to panic. The more you can remember these facts and accommodate your horse's natural way of being, the happier and safer your relationship with your horse will be.

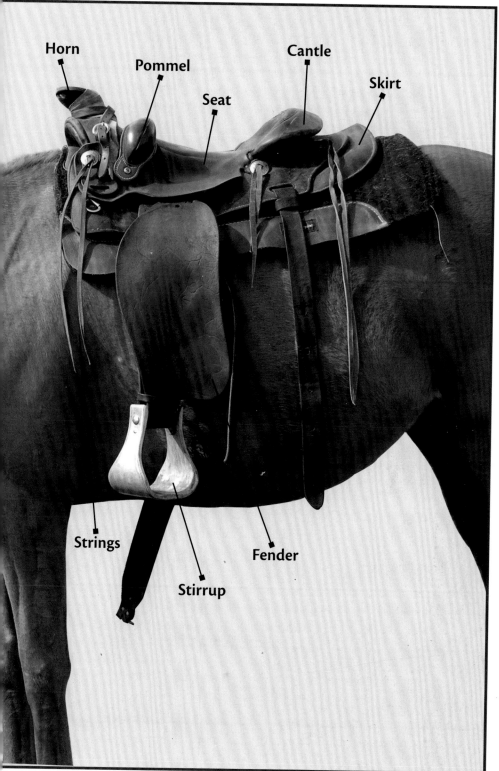

Horn

Pommel

Cantle

Seat

Skirt

Strings

Stirrup

Fender

PREFLIGHT CHECK AND MOUNTING

To avoid getting bucked off a horse when you first ride it, take a lot of time reading the horse. Make sure it is ready for what you are going to be doing with it. The number-one reason people get bucked off on one of their first rides is that they go too fast and ignore what the horse has been trying to tell them. If you get bucked off, you probably missed a lot of signs telling you the buck was coming. This is where being a true horseman or -woman comes into play. It is hard but critical to learn to understand what the horse is feeling emotionally and whether or not you are pushing it too far. Bucking, rearing, and running off are products of a horse being emotionally immature and being pushed too far.

Once you have your horse safely saddled and feel confident in the horse's ability to hold itself together while carrying a saddle, it is time to prepare it for the first ride. In actuality, you have been preparing the horse for the first ride ever since you caught it. If you have been doing a good job with all the different exercises and interactions with your horse, the first ride should be a fairly easy event in its training. It is important to respect the fact that what you are proposing is actually a very big and scary thing for the horse, so make sure you approach this first ride with a lot of respect. There is no set gauge on the amount of time it will take to get the horse ready for its first ride. If you are a good trainer and have a good horse, you may be ready for the first ride within half an hour. If you are a good trainer with a bad horse, it may take months. The best way to make sure you are safe on your first ride is to take too long and get the horse overly prepared.

The first thing I do before mounting a horse, no matter how old or young, is a little groundwork to get a feel for the horse on that particular day. Some days you wake up on the wrong side of the bed; other days you wake up bright eyed, bushy tailed, and happy. The same is true for your horse. Each day is different for the horse. If your horse was really great the last time you had it out, that does not necessarily mean the same greatness will transfer over to today. Yesterday being a good day with your horse is a sign that today might be good, but it is definitely not something you want to bank on. People seem to worry a lot about silly things such as wind, temperature, and lunar cycles and their effects on horses. Although I do believe these things have an effect on horses, I don't believe you should let them. People use weather changes, lunar cycles, and wind as an excuse for a horse's poor behavior. It is never a good idea to make up excuses for horses. Doing this will not help anything and will only make your training longer and more arduous.

This photo shows a preflight check on a horse that has gone through the procedure quite a few times. The horse looks pretty bored with the whole thing and is not at all scared by what the trainer is doing with the rope. A horse that looks like this will be safe to ride. There is no such thing as a horse that is too prepared, so even if your horse is quiet, it does not hurt to refresh its memory from time to time.

Always get the horse to yield its hind end from both sides before mounting.

Once the horse does a nice turn on the forehand, it is good to get the horse to do a nice turn on the haunches.

Make sure that your one-rein stop works from both sides and that the horse is soft and responsive.

The first thing I do before mounting a horse, no matter how old or young, is a little groundwork to get a feel for the horse on that particular day.

Once the preflight check has been completed, we like to send the horse around the trainer in a circle. This allows the horse to really move and to get the saddle feeling comfortable on its back.

The last and arguably most important thing to do is to make sure you have the cinch tight and tied securely. You can avoid a lot of injuries simply by making sure the saddle will not fall off when you are riding. If you are going to be riding for a long time, it is not a bad idea to get off after half an hour or so and retighten your cinch.

To ensure that you are safe the first time you attempt to ride your horse, it is important to do a preflight check. Remember that a pre-ride check is not a substitute for getting your horse in the appropriate mental place prior to attempting to ride. A preflight check is a small group of exercises that helps ensure your horse is in the appropriate state of mind before you climb aboard. The original saying is, "Do a preflight check so you don't take flight." Failure to do a preflight check, no matter how simple, will put you at risk for getting into trouble with your horse. Airplane pilots go through a preflight check to ensure safety and a smooth flight. If anything on the checklist is out of order or not operating correctly, pilots do not start the plane. The same thing applies to you and your horse. If your horse is good on most things during your preflight check but has a few issues, it is not a good idea to attempt to mount the horse or go for a ride. Some people are really good riders and can ride a horse when it bucks. However, most people do not have the ability to ride a bucking horse. I can't, so I make sure my horse is ready and as good as can be before I get on its back.

Start off by saddling your horse and taking it into an arena or open area. As you are leading the horse away from where you have saddled it, watch for any signs of agitation or bucking. If a horse feels overwhelmed by the saddle and wants to buck, it will do so within the first few steps. Once you are in the open area, send your horse around you in a large circle. Make sure to go through all three gaits: walk, trot, and canter. Closely watch the transitions. These are where you will see how the horse is really feeling that day. If the horse tosses its head, bucks, or wrings its tail as it is

doing a transition, you will know something is off with the horse. It is important to pay attention to this. Do not get on a horse that is showing any of these signs during your preflight check. Continue working with the horse on its transitions until they are smooth. Do transitions in both directions, from walk to trot, trot to canter, canter to trot, trot to walk, and walk to stop.

After your horse can smoothly walk, trot, and canter in either direction, make sure your one-rein stop is working well. Make certain it works well on both the left and right side of the horse. Once this is working well, back up a little to make sure the horse is going to back up appropriately. Remember that better backing equals better braking, so if your horse typically has a hard time stopping, it is very important to do a lot of walking backward.

Each horse will require a different preflight check, so tailor your preflight check to your particular horse. If your horse typically bucks from trot to canter, it is incredibly important to make trot-to-canter transitions part of your preflight check. If your horse has a hard time turning or doing one-rein stops, make sure to include these in the preflight check. There is no specific order or schedule of events for a preflight check. Just make sure you feel confident that the horse is mentally and emotionally ready to accept a rider.

Mount your horse only when you know that it is emotionally and mentally prepared. Mount your horse sometimes from the left and sometimes from the right. This way, your horse will not be one-sided, and it will not be a big surprise to the horse if one day you get on the unfamiliar side. There is nothing like being prepared. I once saw a seller at

> Remember that better backing equals better braking, so if your horse typically has a hard time stopping, it is very important to do a lot of walking backward.

When you are ready to mount the horse, it is important to practice mounting from both sides. This way, your horse will be equally developed on both sides and you will run less risk of accidentally scaring it.

an auction trying to show off his horse in the ring. He got on the horse on the left side and dismounted on the right side. The problem was he had never practiced this at home. When the horse saw all 250 pounds of cowboy stepping off on what it thought was the wrong side, it let out a giant fart and jumped sideways, leaving the cowboy behind. The unfortunate part of the story is that the cowboy accidentally got his foot caught in the stirrup and was dragged around the arena by his right boot until people were able to stop the horse. He would have been able to avoid this calamity by preparing the horse on

both sides from the start. Having a one-sided horse is not safe. It is very important that you never have such a "fun" experience with a horse. Make sure you are thorough in all your training so that we do not hear stories like this about you.

Proper Mounting

Start by taking the reins in your left hand and standing on the left side of the horse. Make certain that the left rein is shorter than the right rein. This way, if your horse walks away or starts bucking, you will be able to pull a one-rein stop to halt any bad behavior as soon

Start by putting both reins in your left hand and turning your stirrup so you can get your foot into it.

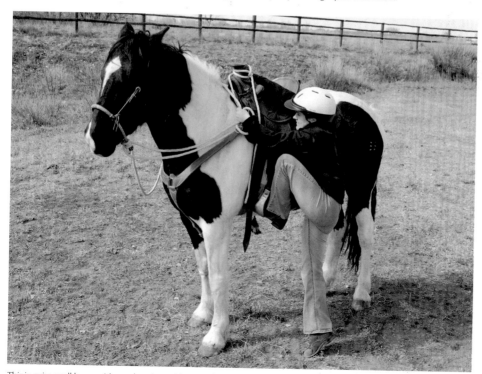

This is quite a tall horse with a rather short rider. It is okay for the rider to hold on to the D-ring on the side of the saddle if that is what it takes for her to be able to get on.

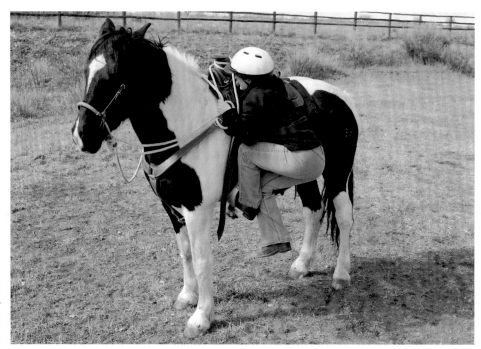

The hardest part of this particular mounting is getting up to the standing position in the stirrup. It is important to not pull on the horse's face or kick it in the belly as you stand up.

As soon as you are fully up in the stirrup, stand for a moment and pet the horse.

as it starts. Stand by the horse's shoulder, facing the rear, and put your left hand on top of the withers to hold your balance. With your right hand, grab the stirrup and turn it so that your left foot can easily slide into it. It is important not to put your whole foot into the stirrup when mounting a horse. This increases your odds of getting hung up if you have to remove it quickly in an emergency. Placing just your toes and the ball of your foot in the stirrup will give you plenty of traction and power, and you can stand up in the stirrup without getting your foot caught if the horse does something unexpected. Place your left foot in the stirrup and reach up with your right hand to grab the right-hand side of the saddle's pommel. Release your left hand from the withers so that it is not pinned down and useless. This hand needs

Once you are all the way in the saddle, allow the horse to stand for a few moments before walking off. This gives you time to get your stirrups placed and get comfortable.

to be free to pull a one-rein stop in case of emergency. At this point, you should be in a fairly odd-looking position, with one hand on the opposite side of the horse on the pommel, one foot in the stirrup, and the other foot on the ground, but your position should also feel fairly stable. Step up into the stirrup with your left foot until you are standing up straight, with your navel over the middle of the horse's back. It is important that you focus on getting your weight over the center of the horse's back as quickly as possible whenever you step up into a saddle. The few moments when you are

pulling yourself up are not very comfortable to your horse, so it is important to make them as quick as possible. Allow your horse to stand still for a second while you are standing up in the one stirrup. Pet the horse on both sides and either step off the horse or swing your leg up and over. The reason for placing your right hand on the pommel and not the back of the saddle is that your hand jerks the horse less when it is on the pommel. You also do not have to reposition your arm to allow your leg to swing over once you are in the standing position. This technique increases your safety,

This is a hazard of trying to get on your horse while holding the cantle with your right hand. The rider is stuck and has to let go of the saddle to swing her leg over.

This is the smart way for a short person to get onto a tall horse. Notice that the stirrup is no longer at the rider's shoulder, and she can now easily step on without hurting herself. Even with a mounting assist like this, it is important to mount in the appropriate order. Just because you are tall does not mean you should change your safe-mounting sequence.

especially when you are riding a horse that may do something unexpected.

Horses that walk away when someone steps on typically do so because of previous riders getting on and riding off into the sunset all in one motion. If you mount your horse step by step, it will never get into the habit of walking away as soon as you step up into the saddle. If you own a horse that starts walking as soon as you step into the stirrup, you can fix this by pulling a one-rein stop as soon as the horse takes a step. As soon as the horse stops, step off the horse. Your horse will quickly realize that you would like it to stand still.

Proper Dismounting

You will want to get off your horse at some point. It is important to dismount in a safe way so as not to create bad habits for the horse. Inappropriate dismounting can lead to a host of problems that are difficult to fix, such as the horse walking off as you are dismounting, so it is best to teach the horse what to do in order for you to correctly dismount from the start. The first step in dismounting is to stop your horse. This advice may sound funny, but you would be amazed how many horse owners do not understand this simple concept. Stop your horse and make it stand for a while. As the

When you are dismounting, especially from a tall horse, swing your leg over the saddle until you are back in the standing position. Hold this position for a moment to make sure the horse is going to stand still.

Lean your belly farther over the horse and pull your foot out of the stirrup.

Push yourself away from the horse and drop down.

horse stands there, pet it and tell it what a good job it just did. Once the horse is fully relaxed, place both your reins in your left hand, with the left rein shorter than the right. This is the same thing you did when you were mounting, so if your horse goes to walk off or does anything to make you nervous, you can pull a one-rein stop with your left hand. Place your right hand on the pommel on the right-hand side of the saddle while watching closely that your horse is staying calm. Lean forward and swing your right leg over the back of the horse until you are back in the standing position you had during the mounting sequence. Now you can step down. Remember to pull most of your left foot out of the stirrup before swinging your right leg over. This way, if the horse jumps sideways or does something silly, your foot will pop out of the stirrup. If you are a short person on a tall horse and you try to simply step off the horse, you will probably get hung up in the stirrup, with one leg dangling a few inches above the ground. Depending on your age and weight—and the stability of your knees—you could have a variety of interesting responses from your body. A nice way to get around this problem is to align your bellybutton a bit farther over the horse while standing in the left stirrup. Pull your left foot out of the stirrup, push yourself away from the horse, and land on both feet. You do not want to slide down the side of the horse. If you do this, you will catch your clothes and possibly injure yourself. Although it may look funny, it's very dangerous when someone hooks his or her shirt when sliding down the horse, is stuck, and has no way of getting free.

> Inappropriate dismounting can lead to a host of problems that are difficult to fix, such as the horse walking off as you are dismounting, so it is best to teach the horse what to do in order for you to correctly dismount from the start.

Riding Posture

To ensure your safety while riding a horse, it is important to have the correct posture and seat. This will help the horse make the appropriate moves and will also help it move its feet safely and freely. A story from the Old West tells of the importance of riding well: A cowboy once rode a horse until it was completely exhausted and lay down to die. The cowboy took his saddle off and left the horse. A Native American came along, got the horse up, and rode it another 10 miles. The cowboy had bounced around and did not ride with the horse. The horse had to work twice as hard to carry him on its back. When he rode, the Native American was almost like an extension of the horse. He was able to get much more out of the horse than the cowboy ever could. We want to ride like the Native American, so that we can get the most out of our horses.

To ride like a true extension of your horse, you must make sure that the length of your stirrups is correct for your height. If your stirrups are too long, you will constantly be falling forward and feel as though the horse is pitching you over its neck. If your stirrups are too short, your legs will be uncomfortable and will cramp easily. The way to check stirrup length is to stand up in the stirrups while you are mounted and check the gap between your seat and the saddle. You should be able to slide your hand vertically in between you and your saddle. I check my stirrups each time I ride, because a horse's size will affect the length of the stirrups. If the horse you are riding is skinny, the stirrups could be longer than usual. If the horse is fat, the stirrups could be shorter than usual. It is important to check your stirrups as soon as you get on the horse.

Learning to ride like a true extension of the horse requires you to ride bareback, so you can truly feel every muscle and movement of the horse. Once you can ride a horse bareback, you will have no problem riding in a saddle. Never practice riding bareback on a young or inexperienced horse. It is best to learn by riding a broke horse that has been ridden a lot and is not likely to spook. As you are riding, focus on developing what is called an independent seat. An independent seat means that your hind end is separate and independent from your legs and your back; your seat is what moves with the horse. The best way to develop an independent seat is to spend a lot of time riding bareback on a nice horse. Try different things and see what makes you feel like you are stuck to the horse. Lift your legs toward your chest and then push them down as far as you can. Lift your toes up and then point them down. Squeeze your legs in and then completely relax them. All these variations will help you realize what best keeps you on the horse. The important thing is to just enjoy the horse, have fun, and pay close attention to what makes you feel solid on the horse and what makes you feel like you are going to fall off.

The first time you mount your horse, your goal should be to safely mount from each side, sit in the middle, and quietly dismount without any reaction from your horse. You do not need to actually ride anywhere the first time you mount your horse. It is good to simply mount, sit up on the horse, pet it, and then dismount. Be sure to develop both sides of the horse. Do not do this mounting practice when the horse is tied up. If you do this, you run the risk of overwhelming the horse and having it do something scary that could injure it or you. It is best to have the horse free and able to move its feet if it needs to.

Before asking your horse to move, make sure your one-rein stop works well from both the ground and the horse's back. This is your emergency brake, and it will come in handy if the horse decides to throw a tantrum or has an issue with you riding it. Once you are on the horse's back, gently ask it to do a one-rein stop from a standstill. You want to duplicate the process you used on the ground, gently applying pressure and asking for a little bit of neck bending on each side. Slowly progress until you can gently pull the horse's head around and the neck bends well on both sides. If you have a one-rein stop that works well, you also have good left and right steering and a good emergency brake.

Another good stopping method is called a cavalry stop or a one-rein stop. It was taught to all horsemen who rode in the cavalry as an emergency stopping tool. You do this stop by riding along and slightly tipping your horse's nose to either the left or the right. For the sake of this explanation, let's say we are tipping the horse's nose to the right. Once the horse's

> Before asking your horse to move, make sure your one-rein stop works well from both the ground and the horse's back. This is your emergency brake, and it will come in handy if the horse decides to throw a tantrum or has an issue with you riding it.

The one-rein stop may feel a little scary when you first pull it from in the saddle. It is important that you sit back and pull it all the way, despite the scary feeling. Do not pull it only partially.

The horse will go around a few times and stop its feet. If you pull a one-rein stop, it is highly relaxing to the horse. A one-rein stop is extremely beneficial in that it takes away a horse's forward motion without taking away its momentum. If you take away a young horse's forward motion by pulling two reins, you run the risk of having it rear up or flip over. You also run the risk of taking away all its forward momentum.

nose is tipped, keep it tipped and slowly apply pressure with the opposing rein, in this case the left. The horse's head should be slightly tipped to the right as you are pulling on both reins. This technique works like a charm. With its neck bent a little bit, the horse is no longer able to continue with forward motion. If you use this stop with even the slightest tip of the horse's head, you will notice that the horse does not stick its head up when you pull on the reins. It will actually stop more quickly and quietly than it would if you simply pulled back evenly with both reins without the tip of its head.

If you want to be a great horseman or -woman, make sure you use the appropriate cues with your horse. A lot of horses get frustrated, and people get bucked off, when riders use inappropriate cues to ask horses for maneuvers. When done wrong, even something as simple as asking the horse to move forward creates frustration on the part of the horse. The horse typically exhibits this frustration in the beginning with pinned ears and swishing of the tail. This leads to the horse running off and bucking. Training a horse to appropriately respond to pressure starts with the appropriate groundwork. When I teach the horse to go forward as I point and chase, it is not to teach it to go forward when I point forward. It is to teach the horse the appropriate response to pressure. All of your groundwork is intended to teach the horse how to think and how to

When doing a cavalry stop, begin by tipping the horse's nose to one side or the other. Here the trainer is tipping the horse's nose to the right.

respond appropriately to pressure, so it knows what to do when you are in the saddle.

When asking a horse to walk forward, it is important to do it in the appropriate way, so as not to create any resentment in the horse. You want to simply think about moving forward and have the horse step quietly without any negative attitude. The first and easiest way to ask a horse to move forward is with a leading rein start. To do a leading rein start, shift your weight to either the left or right. When you shift your weight

The trainer slowly applies pressure with the opposing rein and gets the horse to stop. Notice that the horse did not throw its head up but simply slowed its feet. The head carriage remains the same.

to one side, you automatically free up the horse's opposing foot for moving forward. If you lean to the right, your weight is on the horse's right front foot and encourages it to stay down, freeing the left foot to move forward. If you lean to the right, you have to do your leading rein start to the left. If you lean to the left, your leading rein start will be to the right. You can also do a leading rein start without leaning, but this is not nearly as effective as leaning to one side or the other. Once you have your weight shifted to one side

or the other—let's say to the right—reach out with your left arm with the rein in that hand and apply direct rein pressure. This is called a leading rein start or direct rein. An indirect rein is when you reach your hand straight up toward your body instead of reaching out. This should feel, to your horse, like you are on the ground and leading it forward as you did in lateral longeing. If you have done your groundwork correctly, when you pull a direct rein/leading rein start, the horse will step off in the direction you are leading.

As soon as the horse stopped its feet, the trainer released the pressure and allowed the horse to stand for a moment.

Another way to get your horse to move forward is the squeeze and go. You do this by simply squeezing the horse's body with your legs, all the way to the bottom of your heels, until the horse takes a step forward. A common mistake people make is squeezing with the knees and calves but not all the way down to the bottom of the heels. As you are squeezing, you may realize that your horse

is kind of dull and does not move forward. Some people believe this is a good spot for spurs. Spurs are a very valuable tool but do not help you get your horse to move forward. Spurs are made for sideways and upward motions. People tend to start kicking horses to get them to move forward if spurs are not enough. Instead of kicking your horse, begin making a rhythmical kissing noise and start

133

With the leading rein start, you increase control of every foot of the horse. The trainer is leaning to the left and rear while leading with his right hand and asking for the right front foot to step forward. Notice that this is the foot the horse is moving forward. If you do this exercise correctly, you will be able to pick which hoof you want to move forward.

tapping your knee with your hand. If the horse still is not moving, slowly move your hand to your rear. Keep rhythmically tapping and moving your hand until you are onto the horse's flesh. As you are doing this, maintain the squeezing pressure with your heels. As soon as your hand is back on the horse's hind end, use ask, tell, and follow-through pressure to get the horse to step forward. Do not give the horse one almighty slap on the rear end out of frustration. Rhythmically tap and slowly build up pressure. As soon as the horse takes a step forward, release your heels and stop tapping it on the hind end. Reach forward, pet the horse, and give it a break for a moment. Your horse may learn the lesson quite quickly and start walking or trotting around. Or the horse may simply take a step or two forward and stop. Either way, give the horse a few moments to digest what you have just done. If you are doing this exercise correctly, the horse should quickly realize that your way of asking it to move forward is by squeezing your legs. You will notice that all of these phases go through ask, tell, and follow through. First you ask the horse to go by squeezing with your heels. Then you tell the horse by kissing and smacking your leg. Finally you follow through by tapping the horse on the hind end with your hand. Remember that you tell your horse the most when you stop applying pressure. Both methods of getting your horse moving forward also work well to get the horse to speed up.

There is a common misconception in the horse world that you kiss and kick to make a horse go forward. In actuality, kicking a horse makes it want to go up. If you pretended to be a horse, got on your hands and knees, and had a friend try to get you to go forward, what would be the most natural method to use? I doubt your friend would put his or her hands behind your armpits and give you a good smack or two. This is not a clear signal for forward motion. If your friend did this, you would probably suck up your gut and say, "Ow! What did you do that for?" But if your friend were to smack you on the behind, this would quite clearly tell you to move forward. The moral of the story is to not kick your horse to go forward. Instead, squeeze and chase the horse forward by applying pressure to its rear end. You will notice that once you are on the horse's back, the forward driving zone is the hind end and no longer the front end. If you chased the horse's front end from the saddle, hopefully the horse would do a turn on the haunches.

During the initial ride of your horse, the first few steps are the most dangerous. Your horse might feel overwhelmed and have some kind of fit, so be careful and be ready to pull a one-rein stop if the situation arises. Some people believe that on the first ride, it's appropriate to have the horse step off, ride forward a few feet, stop it with two reins, and back it up. This will kill your horse's momentum and forward movement, which is not a good thing. You'll end up with a horse that rears up and/or flips over. Allow the horse to walk forward gently on a light rein before stopping it. You want your horse to have forward motion and get used to the feeling of moving with you on its back. You do not want to take this feeling away from the horse, because if you do, it is hard to correct. If at any

> **During the initial ride of your horse, the first few steps are the most dangerous. Your horse might feel overwhelmed and have some kind of fit, so be careful and be ready to pull a one-rein stop if the situation arises.**

As we are cantering along, we start to prepare for the stop well in advance of when we actually ask the horse to stop.

When we are ready to stop, we sit down and relax our bodies trying to get the horse to stop its forward motion with our body language.

The horse has slowed down out of a canter and is now at a walk. However, it has not stopped as we had wanted. So, we use our reins to back up our bodies and make the horse stop.

point you feel the horse is going too fast or getting too excited, immediately pull your one-rein stop. The cool thing about one-rein stops is that they do not harm a horse's momentum. Do this exercise until you feel extremely confident in your horse and your horse feels extremely confident under you. Do not leave the round pen, square pen, or arena until you can safely walk, trot, and canter your horse.

There are two different ways to pull a rein: direct rein and indirect rein. You pull a direct rein by reaching out and leading the horse's nose where you want it to go. You pull an indirect rein by pulling toward your body and keeping your hands in close. When you first begin riding a horse, you are going to be doing a lot of direct reining. As your horse develops, you can begin to use indirect reining. Neck reining is an often misunderstood method of steering a horse. People commonly believe that neck reining means putting your rein on the neck of the horse and having it yield away from the pressure, turning its head in response to pressure from the rein on its neck. While it is possible to teach this response to your horse, it is not the correct way of steering. True neck reining uses your whole body to turn the horse. If you want to turn to the left, instead of putting your right rein across the horse's neck, put your right heel into the horse and ask it to step over. Neck reining often does not make sense to the horse, because you are pulling on the right side of the bit while applying rein pressure to the right side of the horse's neck yet intending to have the horse turn left.

The great horseman Pat Parelli came up with a game called Don't Make Me Touch My Reins. In this game, you always use your body first. If the horse still does not understand what you want, then you use your reins. If you want to make a turn while riding, you turn your head first and look in the direction you want to go. Then you turn your

bellybutton in that direction, followed by your legs. If the horse still has not turned, you use your rein to turn the horse. Again, this exercise follows our theme of ask, tell, and follow through. You ask the horse by looking where you want to go. You tell the horse by turning your body where you want to go. You follow through by using the rein to turn the horse where you want to go. If you do this correctly, the horse will eventually turn just off your asking pressure, which is you looking where you want to go.

For stopping, again we will play Don't Make Me Touch My Reins. When riding along, try to get your horse to stop by just using your seat to slow it down. Sit back and down, bringing your energy level down as well. Stay in this position for a few strides and use your reins to stop the horse and back it up a few steps. Give the horse a few moments to rest and start off again. Continue doing this exercise until the horse feels you slow down with your body and slows its feet as well. These subtle cues may feel odd to you at first, but they make the difference between being a good rider and a great one.

Once you feel confident that your horse is quiet and comfortable at the walk, you can add in a trot. Do the trot the same way you did the walk. Start by squeezing your heels into the horse and giving it a leading rein start. If the horse still does not go, rhythmically kiss at it. If need be, reach back and rhythmically tap the horse on its rear.

When you are ready to canter your horse, make sure you are asking for just one or two steps of canter, not expecting to canter around. If your horse isn't in good shape or is poorly balanced, it will have a hard time cantering in a small space, such as a standard round or square pen. It is a good idea at this point to move into an arena or other large pen so that the horse has plenty of room to get the feel of cantering with someone on its back. To

The rider is sitting with his weight to the rear and outside of the turn. This will help encourage the horse to plant that foot and move all of the rest around that foot.

keep your horse under control, you do this in an enclosed area, not in an open field.

Turn on the Forehand

Say you want your horse to do a turn on the forehand to the right. Start by leaning your weight slightly forward and to the left. This will encourage the horse to keep its front planted and will also free up the right hind foot so that it can step away. Reach your leg slightly toward the rear and apply pressure. If the horse takes a step forward, which it probably will, use your reins to stop it and continue applying pressure on the rear. You have done this from the ground in the lateral longeing exercise, and the horse will quickly realize what you want. As soon as the horse takes a step, release your pressure. Continue this process until you have the hind end easily pivoting around the front end. Begin with small steps and move up to asking for a few steps at a time. Once you have a few steps in one direction, switch to the other direction.

Turn on the Haunches

When you are doing a turn on the haunches, it is good to first to make sure your horse knows how to do a turn on the forehand, because the two moves go hand in hand. Start by leaning opposite the direction you wish to turn, just as you did in the leading rein start. To get your horse to turn on the haunches to the left, reach your left hand out to lead the horse's front end over. If the horse stands there, apply pressure with your right leg. You will feel like you are pushing the horse's front end across. As soon as the horse takes one step to the side with its front end, sit up straight and release all pressure. Use your reins to discourage forward motion. A turn on the haunches is actually a backward motion, so don't let the horse walk through it with its hind end. You want to constantly keep the horse back on its haunches. Once you have

a few steps in one direction, switch to the other. Continue this exercise until you have the horse easily pivoting on its hind legs with asking pressure.

Sideways

Sidepassing is not very hard to do once you have your horse trained well on the ground. Sidepassing on the horse is done exactly as you did it from the ground. Point the horse's nose into a fence. Allow the horse to stand there for a moment. When you are ready to ask it to go sideways, take up the slack in your reins so that they are usable but not pulling on the horse's mouth. Say you are sidepassing your horse to the right. Start by leaning to the left. By leaning to the left, you encourage the horse to lift and move its right feet. Apply pressure with your left leg in the spot it naturally hangs. Your horse may turn and try to walk away from the fence. If it does this, keep its nose pointed at the fence and continue applying pressure with your leg until the horse takes a step to the side. The first step your horse will take to the side will most likely be with either the front or the hind end. Remember to release the pressure each time the horse takes a step. If the horse takes a step sideways with its front end first, continue leaning to the left and pull the horse's nose slightly to the left. Apply pressure with your leg, and the horse's hind end should move in alignment with its front. If your horse takes its first step with its hind end, continue leaning to the left and lead the horse's nose out to the right. This encourages the front end to step over. At first, do this move with exaggeration, so the horse will understand what you are doing. As the horse gets better about going sideways, refine your motions and make them more subtle and discreet. If you do this exercise with enough patience and consistency, your horse will quickly be sidepassing like a dream.

This horse is doing what is referred to as a crossfire, where she is cantering with the left lead in the rear and right lead in the front. This is used in upper level dressage, but should not be encouraged in your training level and early riding.

This horse is cantering on the correct lead. She is leading with both the front and the hind left feet.

This horse is cantering on the wrong lead. She is leading with her right feet but should be leading with her left feet.

Once your horse is sidepassing well along the fence, try it out in the open, using a log as a reference point. Once your horse can sidepass well with the log, try it without any reference point. The first thing you will notice is that the horse will try to walk forward whenever you sidepass it. This is okay, but back it up and try to build an invisible wall in front of the horse that it feels it cannot cross. Build the wall by applying rein pressure every time the horse walks forward when you do not want it to.

Cantering Lead

Leads are something that horses do naturally and that people try to force them to do on a whim. When we talk about a horse's lead, we are talking about which two feet in the canter lead the rest of them. Let's say that your horse is traveling to the right in a circle, and you ask it to canter. The horse leads with its left feet. This is called a counter canter, and it is the opposite of what you want. You can use a counter canter in higher-level maneuvers, but at this stage of training, you want the horse to get the appropriate lead for the appropriate direction. A crossfire is when the horse canters with its front feet leading a different direction than its hind feet. This will feel very goofy to you, so make sure you are correctly asking for the lead. This will ensure that you have the appropriate lead on both the front and the hind feet. If you are going to be trail riding or pleasure riding, there is no real need to worry about your horse's leads. You horse has been picking its own leads since it was born, so you really don't need to give it much of a hand. When I am chasing cattle or some similar activity, I typically let the horse pick its own lead, because it knows which lead it is going to need for that particular terrain better than I do. But if you are going to be riding your horse in competition or anything that requires control over the leads, it is good to know how to appropriately ask for them.

> Make sure to not force anything. Keep at it and have fun. Before you know it, you and your horse will be walking, trotting, and cantering around with ease and safety.

If you are traveling to the right, you want the horse to take the right lead. As you are trotting along, sit back and reach out with a direct rein. Lean to the outside of the circle with your leg, putting pressure on the outside. This will free up the horse's inside foot for the lead. This is just what you did for your leading rein start, although at a faster pace. Allow the horse to canter for a while on the lead that you just asked for. If you ask for a lead and the horse gives you the wrong lead or a crossfire, slow it down to a trot and ask again. As soon as the horse gets the correct lead, allow it to canter until it wants to stop cantering. When it is ready to stop cantering and drops down into a trot, slow it down and call it good. Make sure you are getting correct leads going both ways around the circle.

There is no set time frame for how long all this should take. Go by the horse's timeline first and yours second. Make sure to not force anything. Keep at it and have fun. Before you know it, you and your horse will be walking, trotting, and cantering around with ease and safety. Once you are confident in your horse's ability to walk, trot, and canter in an arena or round pen, let the training sink into the horse. A lot of repetition and hours of gently riding around will make the horse solid in a way that nothing else can.

RIDING SAFETY IN AN ARENA AND ON THE TRAILS

Up until this point, you have most likely been riding your horse in an enclosed pen, such as a round pen or arena. Arenas and round pens are great places to build a strong, trusting foundation with your horse. But you probably do not want to spend the rest of your life riding in an arena or round pen, so at some point you have to exit. This can be a daunting task for many people, because the horse feels very free and therefore a bit out of control at first. You will notice that the first time you ride your horse out of an enclosed area, the horse will move with a whole new

spring in its step. This is a good thing. It is like going for a walk when you have somewhere fun to go. The thing to do is to learn how to control this emotion in your horse and not completely remove it. When you first leave the arena or round pen, make sure you do it on foot and not on horseback. As soon as you are out in the open, treat your horse like a brand-new horse with which you are starting over. Most horses will act differently in the open than in an arena. They are usually less relaxed and less quiet in the open. It is important to do your groundwork in this new open area until the horse is fully relaxed and has fully accepted the feeling of being out in the open with the potential to run for miles.

Once you have your horse ready to ride in the open, make sure you do not ride nervously. Your nervousness will transfer to the horse. Being nervous is a completely natural thing when you are riding a horse, especially if the horse is nervous. The problem occurs when your nervousness makes your horse more nervous, and it will. As your horse is getting more nervous, it will make you more nervous, and your nervousness will make

Riding bareback can help your feet and balance. The more you ride bareback, the better you seat will become and the closer to your horse you will be. It is important to start off slowly on a well-seasoned horse. You might realize quite quickly that you don't have a very good seat. It's ok if you realize this—just stick with it and continue bettering yourself.

When you are riding, it is extremely easy to get nervous and go into the fetal position. The fetal position is when you lean forward and suck your knees towards your chest. The bad thing about doing this is that it puts your weight too far onto the front of the horse, putting you off balance. This makes it so that if the horse were to stop or turn suddenly, it is much easier for you to fall off. It is important to stay leaning back and balancing well.

the horse more nervous. This is a vicious cycle that must be broken by you. If you do not break the cycle, you and the horse will constantly be feeding off one another and will be nervous wrecks within the first few steps of riding in the open. It is very important to control your emotions as you ride your horse. This takes a lot of maturity on your part. You need to look at your fear and say, "I am not going to let you take control of me." There are several telltale signs of nervousness. You will notice tension through your back and legs

and leaning forward with your knees up. For some reason, all humans do this when they begin to feel nervous on a horse. This does not help you ride a horse. Bending forward with your knees coming toward you is a very weak position. If the horse were to do something, you would be on the ground before you knew it, because you have moved your center of gravity too far forward, out of alignment with the rest of your body. If you feel yourself start to go into a fetal position from nervousness,

Some people try to keep their feet off a horse by sticking them out. This is incorrect. Having your legs to the outside will throw off your balance and make it impossible to ride with an independent seat.

This is how you want your legs to look as you are riding. They should be completely relaxed on the horse.

control your emotion, relax your body, sit back, and put your legs down. This is the safest thing to do to ensure that you will not get bucked off. This will also be very relaxing for your horse, because it will feel your emotion come down. Instead of the horse feeding off your nervousness, it will feed off your relaxation and become more relaxed.

Another important element of riding safety, besides keeping yourself emotionally in control, is knowing how and when to use your one-rein stop. As we have said before, the one-rein stop is your emergency break. It has saved many lives. It disengages the hind end of the horse when it is scared, causing the horse to slow its feet and think. When horses are afraid and running off the fear side of their brains, their most natural reaction is to straighten their bodies and keep them as straight as possible. By pulling a one-rein stop, we force the hind end to disengage and stop the horse's natural reaction. It also takes the horse back into a responsive state of mind. You already know how to pull a one-rein stop. Do it whenever you possibly need to. Do not be bashful with pulling a one-rein stop. It is okay to pull one and then look back and say, "I probably did not need to do that." It is better to be safe than sorry.

Another element of riding safety is safety in a group of horses. The best rule when riding with a group is to never trust another person's horse or to simply take someone's word that his or her horse will not kick. I have seen horses kick people after the owner has just said, "This horse never kicks." Be sure

> **If you feel yourself start to go into a fetal position from nervousness, control your emotion, relax your body, sit back, and put your legs down. This is the safest thing to do to ensure that you will not get bucked off. This will also be very relaxing for your horse, because it will feel your emotion come down.**

to exercise caution until the horse proves to you that it is safe and will not kick. If I am riding with a friend I have not ridden with before, I will not let the horses have their own little meet and greet. This is a great opportunity to get pawed in the belly or have someone get kicked. You never see two horses come together for the first time and simply sniff each other and then walk away. They always sniff each other, squeal, and try to form some sort of dominance over one another. This is not something you want to be a part of or try to stand and hold your horse through. If you want horses to meet each other, it is best to put the horses in separate pens that are touching each other with tall fences in between, so the horses can establish dominance without actually touching each other.

As you are riding, you will notice that horses are extremely social and will get to know each other in a safe and calm manner. If you are riding on a trail or out in the open—or anyplace for that matter—it is considered extremely bad manners to ride up behind someone any closer than one horse length away. Horse people often measure distances with horse lengths and horse widths. One horse length is equal to the length of your horse from nose hair to tail hair. One horse width is the distance from one side of the horse to the other. A simple way to tell if you are one horse length behind the horse in front of you is to look between your horse's ears. If you can see the rear feet of the horse in front of you, you are okay. If you cannot, you

Notice the dynamic between the bay and chestnut horses. This meeting is not safe, because you do not know what is going to happen next.

are too close and should give the other horse more space. Think of each horse as having its own personal bubble that you do not want to pop. As you ride with the same horses more often, and they grow more accustomed to one another, you can start riding closer, and their personal bubbles will begin to shrink. Initially, think of each horse's personal bubble as being quite large, just as you would when meeting a person for the first time. Personal space is extremely important to both horses and humans.

Gates often provide an interesting complication, especially when you are on a young or inexperienced horse. Your best bet is to have the person with the most experienced horse take care of the gate, especially if you are a long distance from home. When you are at home on an inexperienced horse, it is a great idea to get the horse used to gates. But when you are out and about and a long way from home, it is best to stay safely in your saddle and allow someone else to open and close the gate. Hang back away from the gate, allowing the more experienced horse and rider to go up to the gate. Once the gate has been opened, ride through but do not continue going down the trail or ride away from the horse and rider who have just stopped to get the gate. This is extremely poor manners and will make the horse that is left behind panic and think that its herd of protection is leaving. A very interesting psychological side note is that a horse feels better leaving its friends behind than being left behind by its friends. Make sure to keep this on your mental radar so you can be extra safe, cautious, and considerate of others as you are riding. If you are riding with others and they leave you behind as you are getting the gate, feel free to inform them that this is not appropriate behavior. Do not be too shy to say that these riders are making your life dangerous. It is better to tell them and stay safe than not tell them and risk getting yourself injured.

Hand in hand with a horse fearing being left behind by its friends is a mental condition called barn sour. Whenever it is away from its pen or its buddies, a horse with barn sour has some form of fit and wants desperately to return to the barn. Barn sour can exhibit itself in many different ways—not just in nervousness when the horse is away from the barn. Barn sour may come in the form of the horse prancing on the way home, stopping, and no longer wanting to continue walking away from home, or changing speed when headed home. Any one of these behaviors is a problem and should be addressed. Remember that this behavior is a symptom and not a disease. We need to figure out what is causing the anxiety about being away from the barn and making the horse wish to be home so badly. With barn sourness, 99 percent of the time, the horse-to-human relationship has some kind of issue. The horse does not see the human as a leader or companion it is comfortable being around in a dangerous environment. Remember how the misbehaving young horse felt when it was pushed away from the herd. It makes a horse highly anxious to feel it is all alone and vulnerable to attack. I see people trying to

fix barn sourness by taking a horse out, away from its buddies, and longeing it in circles until it is very tired. Or they take the horse out by itself, tie it up, and leave it for a long time until it no longer misses its friends. None of these methods works in the long run, and they will only cause increased anxiety in the horse. If you want to fix barn sour, fix the way the horse sees you and your relationship with it. The wild horse felt better as soon as it was back with the lead mare; you want your horse to feel the same way about you. This may require going back to the basics and taking extra time to build the relationship, but this work is worth it to help the horse be more confident away from home.

When you are planning to go trail riding, it is a good idea to scout the area in which you will be riding before you take your young or inexperienced horse out. A good first-trail-ride trail will be mostly flat and not have too many obstacles. There is nothing fun about going trail riding and reaching a bridge or river crossing that your horse is not ready for and refuses to cross. It is good to first ensure that there is nothing about the trail that will be too tricky or overwhelming for your horse. It is good to note whether or not this is a highly trafficked bicycle, foot, or horse trail. It is not a big deal if it is a bike or pedestrian trail, as long as you are prepared. You do not want to take your horse onto a trail that it is not prepared for, so if there are going to be a lot of bikes, practice at home. Make sure your horse has seen a bicycle, has had one ride by it, and is comfortable with the idea of being passed by one. It is also important to remember that the general public does not have any knowledge of horses. Do not expect people to know what to do to keep you safe. Instead, make sure you have your horse fully prepared. If you see cyclists on the trail, greet them and feel free to ask them to move

This horse desperately wants to get back with its friends. It is extremely barn sour and going so far as to canter sideways to get back to the barn. If you encounter a horse that does this, relax, stay with it, and continue trying to get its attention.

off to the side of the trail or to slow down. Make sure you are aware of what is going on around you. If a cyclist is coming up behind you, take your horse off the trail and turn it around so it can face the person coming toward you.

After you have selected the appropriate destination for your trail ride, you need to choose the right people and horses to go with you. You do not want to ride a trail for the first time with someone whose horse is acting nutty or nervous. Make sure you know the

Doesn't this look like a good spot for a first trail ride?

horses you are going to be riding with and that they will be nice, quiet companions for your horse. It is also important that the people riding their horses with you be on the same page. That is, they need to know you are there with your horse for the first time and this is a training endeavor. The first time you go for a trail ride, you and your horse will have no fun if you are with people who have an agenda or are in a hurry. If their idea for the trail ride does not line up with yours, someone is going to end up frustrated. Either you will end up feeling rushed, which is detrimental to your horse's training, or the others will feel you are slowing them down and ruining their fun. Having a quiet and calm companion for your young horse on its first trail ride is a very valuable thing. Your horse will feel more secure having another horse there. A quiet

horse will have a relaxing effect on your horse. The last important thing to look at before going on a trail ride is yourself as a rider. Remember that you are here to have a good time and create a positive experience for your horse. If you have any agenda, such as to run up the hill or cover a certain number of miles, you will have a negative effect on your horse. As long as you keep all these things in your mind as you are riding, your first trail-riding experience should be a positive one for both you and your horse.

Once you get the horse into the trailer, even if it takes five hours, allow the horse a few minutes to stand on the trailer while you pet it. Then turn it around and lead it off the trailer. If you lead the horse on, tie it up, and start heading off to your destination, you will only confirm its fears about you

After your horse has built up its confidence following the bike, begin trotting up and past the bike, then stopping and allowing the bike to pass you. If the bike scares your horse as it comes by, remember to point the horse at the bike. It is important that the horse be allowed to look at what is scaring it.

If your horse is scared of bicycles, enlist a good friend to help get the horse over its fear. Begin by having the horse follow the bicycle. This will increase the horse's confidence that the bicycle is nothing to be afraid of.

and the trailer, making it twice as hard to get the horse on the trailer the next time. Load and unload the horse twenty times before you actually leave it in the trailer and go somewhere. It is important that loading be a part of your normal training and not something you do twenty minutes before you need to be at your destination. Give yourself an entire day to get the horse used to the idea of being loaded and unloaded. It is nice to have some grain or hay ready for the horse once it is in the trailer. This food will help form good memories and give the horse a bit of positive reinforcement once it gets into the trailer. As soon as the horse has had a moment to eat and realize that the trailer is safe, take it back off the trailer. Repetition is key to continued success in trailer loading. Even if you have a horse that you haul all the

time and that has no trouble getting into the trailer, it is still good to load it, pet it for a while, and then unload it.

A horse might be hard to load if it is scared of the way you drive. If you notice that your horse is becoming progressively harder to load, look at your driving habits. Imagine that your center of gravity is way above your feet, and imagine riding around sharp corners with quick acceleration and quick braking. You would constantly feel like you were falling over and not appreciate the vehicle in which you were riding. You would also have no desire to return to the situation that caused you grief. A good exercise to help you truly appreciate how your horse feels about your trailer is to step into the trailer, close it up, and have a friend give you a short ride around the farm. See how it feels to be where

continued on page 159

What if . . . my horse will not load into the trailer?

You will quickly realize that you cannot go trail riding on a horse if your horse does not want to load into the trailer. Typically, when you go to load the horse into the trailer, it will stop hard as soon as it realizes what you are thinking. The horse will lift up its head and back up.

People try many different things to get horses into trailers. I have seen people drag horses in with a truck and push horses in. I have even seen four big, burly guys pick up a horse and put it into a trailer. The typical response of a human is to back the horse up, turn it around, and lead it to the trailer again. But this just teaches the horse that if it stops, looks at the trailer, and backs up, the human will change his or her mind and take it away from the trailer. This was the goal of the horse in the first place, which makes your problem of getting the horse on the trailer worse.

If your horse stops while looking at the trailer and will not move forward, the only correct answer is to hold pressure on the rope until the horse takes a step forward. As soon as the horse steps forward, even with slightest of steps, release the pressure. Allow it to stand for a moment and then apply pressure again, until the horse steps forward again.

Be sure to give your horse a lot of time to think about and look at the trailer. As soon as the horse steps forward, release the pressure. Continue doing this until the horse steps into the trailer.

You want to make sure your horse trailer looks as inviting as possible, so do not open the door just a little and ask the horse to get in. Open the door as far as possible.

This may take a while, but it is the only way to get your horse to gently come into the trailer.

If your horse gets up to the trailer and is about to put one foot in but backs up hard, keep constant pressure on the rope. You will need to move your feet to stay with the horse. Go backward with it until its feet stop and it takes a step forward. As soon as it takes a step forward, release all the pressure.

Do not drag the horse forward. Give the horse a moment and lead it forward again. It is extremely important not to lose your patience while loading a horse on a trailer. Impatience is the reason so many horses are hard to load. As soon as you lose your patience, you stop understanding your horse's prey mentality and start acting like a predator. This makes you even harder for your horse to understand. Remain calm and remember that this is a learning experience for both you and your horse.

The best way to make this an easy experience is to set reasonable goals for your horse before you start to load it. If your horse is really scared of the trailer, perhaps your goal for the first day will be to get the horse within 10 feet of the trailer. The way you get into trouble is by getting too goal oriented. Focus on the principle, and the goal will come. If you focus on the goal, you will forget about the principle and never achieve your goal.

As the horse gives in to you even a little bit, release the pressure. Do not drag the horse into the trailer. It is important that you stay out of the horse's way as it goes into the trailer. You do not want to accidentally block the horse as it goes in.

continued on page 158

As soon as the horse steps its front end into the trailer, the trainer gives the horse a few moments and a lot of petting. This helps tell the horse that it has done the right thing.

Sometimes it is hardest to get the horse's back feet into the trailer. Be patient and persistent. The horse will go in.

continued from page 155

your horse is riding. This is not a legal or safe exercise to do on public roads, so do it on your farm or in a parking lot. Once you know what it feels like to be in the back of a trailer, you will have a whole new appreciation for how your horse feels and will definitely modify the way you drive. If you accidentally take sharp turns or use your brakes hard from time to time, it is forgivable. However, constant fast and reckless driving will lead to horses having a great fear of riding in your trailer.

Before you leave your home for a trail ride, or any ride, it is important to make a checklist of things to bring, so that you don't accidentally forget an important item. There is nothing worse than driving all the way to where you are going to ride and realizing that you have forgotten your bridle, saddle, or other important item. A simple and easy way to avoid these mistakes is to make a checklist of things to bring on the ride. I made my checklist on laminated paper and hung it inside the door of my trailer. I mark items off with a dry erase marker as I place them in the trailer. I erase the previous trip's marks and start over the next time.

Safety is extremely important, especially when heading out to the trail, the woods, or scarcely populated areas. We are always worried about the emotional well-being of our horses and ourselves, but there is also a

continued on page 167

A more advanced way of loading your horse into the trailer is by standing at the door and sending it in the same way you would send it around in a circle.

As soon as the horse makes an effort, leave it alone, even if it is not what you consider a big effort.

As soon as the front feet step up and in, be sure to give the horse lots of pets and praise. This horse is doing what we are asking it to do, but doing it rather unconfidently. It is important to reassure the horse that it is doing the right thing and is safe.

Once the horse has had a moment to rest, ask it to go the rest of the way into the trailer. Often, the horse will not step into the trailer with the hind end. It will jump.

There are two acceptable ways of getting your horse off the trailer. The first is by backing it off. The second is to turn the horse around and allow it to walk off. Remember that if you allow the horse to turn around and walk off the trailer, it shouldn't come off too fast because it could hurt itself.

What if . . . my horse does not want to cross water?

It is a bad thing if your horse takes one look at a water crossing, turns, and heads for the trailer. The way to fix this problem is to keep facing the water.

Do not let the horse turn around and walk away from the water, just as you did not allow the horse to turn around and walk away from the

trailer when you were having problems trailer loading. Giving in allows the horse to win and makes it even harder to get it to cross the water.

If you kick your horse, which is a natural reaction to the frustration, you will make the horse go into reverse or up. Simply sit back, relax, and keep the horse's nose pointed at the water.

When your horse first approaches water, prepare to stop. The horse will likely step up to the water, stop, and back up. It's important that you're not leaning forward, so you don't fall off the front of the horse when it backs up.

As soon as this horse realized what the rider was doing, it tried to run sideways, away from the water. The trainer needs to stay relaxed and keep the horse's nose pointed straight at the water, so the horse does not get away from it.

If your horse takes a step forward, pet it on the neck and allow it to stand and look at the water for a moment.

Do not force the horse into the water. Keep gently asking the horse to step across and keep it pointed at the water. No matter what the horse does to try to get away, keep its nose pointed at the water. If you are gentle enough, the horse will eventually become curious and step into the water. Make sure you stop pushing it as soon as it steps in the water.

When they do not want to cross water, most horses tend to throw it into reverse, back up fast, and try to scare the rider into turning away from the water. Allow your horse to back up as far as it needs to. As soon as the horse stops, reward it

continued on page 164

and ask it to move forward again. If you do not force the horse the first time it steps into the water, it will do just that—step, not jump, in the water.

A lot of people have trouble with their horses going up to water, looking at it, snorting at it, and jumping over it. If you slow down and gently get the horse to step up to the water, the horse will step into it instead of jumping over or into it. Once your horse is in the water, allow it to paw and sniff the water all it wants. This is a great time to gently pet the horse and reassure it. As soon as the horse loses interest in the water, you are free to ask it to continue moving.

As soon as the horse turns, faces the water, and stops trying to get away from it, the trainer releases all pressure and allows the horse to stand for a moment.

After the horse has had a moment to relax, the trainer asks the horse to step forward again. Notice the change in the horse's posture and overall excitement level. It is very relaxing for the horse when you have the good timing and sense to stop pressuring it and allow it a moment to rest. The horse has calmed down quite a bit and gently steps into the water.

As soon as the horse is fully in the water, the trainer pets it and gives it some time to relax and play with the water.

What if . . . my horse will not cross a bridge?

Bridge crossings are a lot like water crossings, only they are much more dangerous. Bridge crossings are extra dangerous because you are giving your horse a narrow walkway where it is safe to go only forward or backward, not side to side.

If the horse steps onto the bridge and gets scared by something on its left or right, it will jump into the water or ravine that you are crossing. There is a reason that the bridge is where it is. The water is probably not safe, or the ravine is too big or in some way dangerous. You do not want your horse jumping off a bridge.

When training your horse on bridges, start off on a bridge that is safe and low, so that if the horse steps off the bridge to the side, you do not have to worry about it hurting its legs or feet. When first introducing your horse to the bridge, it is a good idea to do so with your feet on the ground. Unless you are a great rider, it is not a good idea to ride a horse over a bridge the first time. If you are on the ground, the horse can move its feet if it gets overwhelmed or scared, and you won't get hurt.

Treat crossing bridges the same way you treat trailer loading. Go across the bridge and leave your horse on the other side. Turn around and face the horse. Lead the horse forward. Each time it takes a step forward, reward it by releasing the pressure on the lead rope. If your horse starts to sniff the bridge or paw at it, allow this for as long as it wants, with absolutely no pressure on your part. As soon as the horse quits sniffing or pawing at the bridge, gently ask it to walk forward. As soon as the horse steps onto the bridge, allow it to stand there for a bit and relax. Continue doing this until the horse walks across and gets to you on the other side. As soon as the horse gets to you, it is time for a lot of petting and praising. Continue praising the horse and leading it across the bridge until it walks across as if the bridge were not even there.

It may take a lot of time to get the horse crossing bridges quietly, but it is definitely well worth your time and effort. Once you can safely lead your horse across the bridge, it is safe to ride across. Make sure you stay relaxed and focused on getting to the other side as you ride across the bridge. This will help your horse get across as efficiently and safely as possible. You will increase your horse's anxiety if you are anxious when you ride. Tell yourself to relax and sit back. This will be very calming for your horse.

Do not allow the horse to go halfway and stop and stand for a while, because you increase the odds of something coming up and scaring it, making it want to jump off the bridge. You can also make the horse anxious about bridges by forcing it across the bridge too quickly. It is a delicate balance, so use good judgment.

continued from page 159

physical element to think of, especially when you are leaving home. A good first-aid kit for both you and your horse can save both your lives on the trail. Even a short ride into the mountains can be disastrous if you do not have the appropriate medical supplies to help yourself or your horse. Most tack stores sell a nice horse/human first-aid kit that straps onto the saddle. The only problem with strapping the first-aid kit to your saddle is that if you get bucked off your horse, you won't have the first-aid kit. It is a good idea to keep your first-aid kit in a small backpack, so if you are bucked off, you will have your supplies with you and not attached to the saddle. Horse/human first-aid kits have the necessary equipment to repair you or your horse in an emergency. They do not have everything that a veterinarian has, but they have enough to help with most emergency situations.

You also need to keep yourself physically safe while riding in the backcountry. The most fragile and important part of your body is your head. It is easy to protect your head by wearing a helmet. If you are insecure or nervous, even the slightest bit, it is a good idea to protect your head. A helmet is a cheap insurance policy against the damage and lasting effects that come from a brain injury. A bike helmet is not the same as a horse helmet. Horse helmets cover more of the back of your head than bike helmets. The fit of the helmet is extremely important in its ability to provide the needed protection. When you shake your head with the helmet on, the

> Safety is extremely important, especially when heading out to the trail, the woods, or scarcely populated areas. We are always worried about the emotional well-being of our horses and ourselves, but there is also a physical element to think of, especially when you are leaving home.

helmet should not move at all. Most helmets come with additional padding that can snug up the fit if it's loose. The straps should be snug against your chin and face. Remember, it is not what you put on your head, it's what you put in it. This means that a helmet is not an excuse for poor horsemanship. In addition, sun protection, appropriate clothing in layers, and the right amount of food and water will ensure that you feel good through your whole ride and come back safely. Hope for the best but plan for the worst, and you will have an enjoyable and safe time.

As you are riding on the trail, you will encounter all sorts of interesting obstacles that will provide good training moments with your horse. Whether you encounter a bridge, a river, or wildlife, it is important to stay relaxed and calm and to remember that this is a training trip. Do not be offended if your horse gets nervous or does something wrong. Remember when you were growing up. You made some mistakes, but overall you were a good person. The same is true of the horse. If it steps out of line and makes a mistake or two, it is okay. The horse is mentally young and still learning.

Everything in this book is the foundation for success in specialized areas. If you don't build a strong foundation, you can never truly have any specialization. Our goal is for you to be foundation people who form happy horse/human relationships before progressing on to specialization for competition. This book is intended to be an overall starting place for you and your horse

What if . . . my horse is afraid of wildlife?

It's completely natural for a horse to be afraid of wildlife and farm animals such as alpacas, llamas, chickens, and sheep. Unfortunately, unless you own a wild animal menagerie or have a highly trafficked wildlife area in your backyard, there is no great way to desensitize your horse to wildlife—because you cannot predict where your horse will encounter wild animals.

The best thing to do is to develop your horse and help it lose other fears, such as its fear of cars, motorcycles, bicycles, flags, plastic bags, and tarps, which appear in more predictable situations. If your horse has no fear of these things, chances are it will have no problem with wildlife.

As you are training, you are not just teaching your horse not to be afraid of tarps, bags, or flags; you are actually teaching the horse how to deal with its fear and cope when it is afraid. If you have taught your horse how to cope and control itself when it is afraid, you will have no problem with a little bit of wildlife.

When a horse is really scared of something, it will raise its head as high as possible, tip its nose out, point both ears forward intently, and look at whatever it is that is scaring it. This posture is the international horse sign for "There is something over there that might try to eat me." If your horse sees another animal looking off in the distance with this expression, it will get scared. This is partially why deer, llamas, alpacas, and elks are so scary to horses. When a deer looks straight at a horse with what is a relaxed expression for the deer, the horse reads it as a very scared horse and picks up on the fear.

Helmets are extremely important safety gear. If you feel you need one, it should be worn at all times. Some people believe that every rider should wear a helmet no matter what and that the government should enforce the rule. I say it is up to each person to decide for him- or herself what feels safe and unsafe. The great thing about modern helmets is that they are unique and quite fashionable, giving the rider a fun way to express him- or herself.

as you are on your horsemanship journey. Continuing education is the best possible thing you can do. Learn from any masters you can find, and try to learn as much from your horse as you possibly can. Here's hoping that your education never stops. Be safe, have fun, and don't take yourself too seriously. Happy trails.

GLOSSARY

bosal: a rawhide noseband used to make a hackamore

cantle: the part of your saddle that keeps you from sliding off the rear when the horse moves forward. Cantles can be short or tall, depending on the saddle. We prefer a cantle that is right in between. If your cantle is too tall, it will push you too far forward. If there is no cantle, you are likely to fall off if the horse jumps forward.

Cheyenne roll: a roll put on the cantle of your saddle. The Cheyenne roll is extremely handy, because if the horse starts to buck, you can hold onto it and keep your butt down in the saddle.

dressage: a Renaissance-period sport used to showcase a high level of partnership between horse and human through a progressive training system. Dressage has different skill levels, from beginner to Olympic. Riders can compete against people of the same level. If you enter a level-one dressage show, you will compete against other level-one riders. The bad thing about a lot of horse sports is that the first time you compete, you are competing at the highest level of competition. Dressage allows you to compete from start to finish against people with a similar skill level.

driving: one of two different sports. Pleasure driving is just what it sounds like—driving a horse for pleasure. This is a noncompetitive sport and is usually centered on relaxed afternoon drives with friends. The second form of driving, competitive driving, has several different aspects. You can do competitive driving dressage, which is a lot like low-level riding dressage. You can also do cones, trying to drive through a course as perfectly as possible. Another option is the marathon, the most exciting level of competitive driving. The marathon course is set up over many miles. Teams travel between obstacles. You trot your horse to an obstacle and try to make it through as quickly as you can. Then you trot on to the next obstacle. It takes a lot of skill not to overspend your horse's energy too soon. Another aspect of competitive driving is show-ring driving, in which you go into the arena with your hitch of one to eight horses and drive around. You are judged on your quality of driving, as well as the harness, horse, and wagon.

endurance racing/competitive trail riding: very intense competitions. People often think these are soft sports that do not require the training or sheer bravery that some other competitions require. But these competitions are actually are very intense. Some competitive trail rides are 50 miles or more, all on the same horse. You ride a course through open fields, across ditches, over rocks, and up mountains, with health checks every few miles. Both horse and human have to be in intensely good shape to compete in and survive one of these events. Training for an event is long and arduous.

fiador: a special knot tied into a length of parachute cord that is paired with a hackamore. The fiador acts as a throat latch and keeps the hackamore from popping off over the horse's nose.

horse measuring: measuring a horse from the ground to the highest point on its withers. This measurement is taken in units called hands. One hand equals four inches.

hackamore: a tool made with a bosal noseband, a hanger to keep the noseband in place, mecate reins, and possibly a fiador. The hackamore is a traditional Spanish riding tool that is popular today in developing bridle horses.

half-breed bit: a bit that resembles a spade bit but that does not have a spoon. This bit is a little easier to get your horse to embrace. It requires that you use a curb strap as well.

jumping: an exciting sport that requires exacting skill mixed with a little bit of daring. Jumps can be as low as 6 inches or as high as 8 feet, with standard jumps in the 4- to 6-foot range. The official world record for height is 8 feet, 1.25 inches. This sport presents an interesting challenge for horse and rider. It is a bit punishing on the horse. Eventually, the horse will say, "I'm done going over these jumps." The rider has to find a way to make the horse want to jump without feeling as though it is being forced.

pommel: the part of the saddle that is right in front of your legs and connects to the horn. An easy way to remember this name is to remember that the pommel is where your palms go.

reining: A competition that shows off the speed and agility of a Western horse. Horses are asked to canter as fast as they can, slide stop, stand for a moment, and do a quick turn on the haunches into a canter. They are also asked to stop hard, turn hard, and spin while holding perfect body position. This is a very exacting sport in the same way dressage is a very exacting sport. It takes lots of time and energy to get the horse to turn and stop with the kind of perfection that will win competitions.

rodeo events: calf roping, steer wrestling, barrel racing, pole bending, and other competitions. Rodeo is the number-one place where the public encounters horses. Rodeo also happens to be the number-one place where people put their competitive desires ahead of their relationships with horses. Rodeo was originally intended to show off the high level of partnership between horse and human in a ranch setting and how they could do an impressive job of ranch work together. Modern-day rodeos, although impressive, have lost most of the relational aspects. A few people still stress their relationship to the horse in this kind of competition, but they are the exception and not the rule. It's interesting to note that people who stress the relationship with the horse are usually the ones who win.

snaffle bit: any bit that does not have leverage. The bit does not necessarily have to break in the middle to be considered a snaffle. The snaffle bit is the most common bit in the horse world.

spade bit: a shanked bit that has an elaborate mouthpiece. The mouthpiece includes a hooded or unhooded roller and a spoon. This bit must be used with a curb strap. It looks extremely severe because it goes so far into the horse's mouth. The bit itself is not severe, although the way some people use it is. The spade bit is historically a vaquero bit.

three-day eventing: an intense and demanding competition that requires riders to master three different skills: dressage, cross-country riding, and stadium jumping. Three-day eventing has its roots in military training and was first called the Militaire.

© Eric Gevaert/Shutterstock

RESOURCES

Books:

Farming with Horses, Steve Bowers

The Faraway Horses, Buck Brannaman

True Horsemanship through Feel, Bill
  Dorrance and Leslie Desmond

*Ranch Horsemanship: How to Ride Like the
  Cowboys Do*, Curt Pate

Troubleshooting!, John Lyons

Videos:

Turning Loose with Ray Hunt, Ray Hunt

Colt Starting with Ray Hunt, Ray Hunt

*Clinton Anderson: On the Road to the Horse
  Colt Starting Championship*, Clinton
  Anderson

Gaining Respect & Control on the Ground,
  Clinton Anderson

Websites:

Nathan Bowers: bowersfarm.com

Pat Parelli: parelli.com

Josh Lyons: www.lyonslegacy.com

Tack:

287 Supply

120 North U.S. Highway 287

Fort Collins, CO 80524

(970) 493-7322

Horsefriendly.com

© Nic Neish/Shutterstock

INDEX

About the Authors

Katie Bowers Reiff has been photographing the West for the past 10 years while learning about horses from her dad and brother. She lives in northern Colorado with her husband. They run a vehicle graphic design company together.

Nathan Bowers has been training horses for the public for the past 12 years. He got his start learning how to train difficult horses from his dad. He travels around the world teaching other people how to get along with their horses. He lives on the family ranch near Fort Collins, Colorado.